The Piano Handbook

The Piano Handbook

Ian McCombie

DAVID & CHARLES
Newton Abbot London

British Library Cataloguing in Publication Data

McCombie, Ian K.
  The piano handbook
  1. Piano – Maintenance and repair
  I. Title
  786.2'3   ML652

  ISBN 0–7153–7931–3

First published 1980
Second impression 1980
Third impression 1983

Typeset by Trade Linotype Ltd, Birmingham
and printed in Great Britain
by Biddles Limited, Guildford, Surrey
for David & Charles (Publishers) Limited
Brunel House   Newton Abbot   Devon

Contents

Acknowledgements

The author appreciates the help given by the staff at Williams Piano House Ltd, Vancouver, in particular Mr Norman May, Mr Albert Alexander and Mr Bruce Nolan, in the preparation of photographs. He also wishes to thank the Baldwin Piano and Organ Company, Cincinnati, the Kawai America Corporation, Los Angeles, and Welmar Pianos Ltd, London, for providing illustrations, and is most grateful for the encouragement and help of Mr Renato Lentini, tuner-technician, Vancouver.

The drawings are by Dave Thompson, West Vancouver, and June Sherwood, Sechelt, British Columbia.

Part One
Basic Information

1 Early Pianos

When your little girl plays the piano she is indebted to Bartolomeo Cristofori, who, like a fairy godmother, changed a harpsichord into a piano nearly three hundred years ago.

Cristofori was a builder of fine harpsichords in Florence, where he worked under the patronage of the wealthy Ferdinando de Medici. He realised that when he became angry and frustrated, or even when he felt enthusiastic, and banged on the keys, the harpsichord did not respond with satisfactory crashing chords, but with delicate sweet tones. It could play neither very softly nor loudly: it was a tranquil instrument suitable only for the elegant drawing-rooms of the rich.

The single strings of the harpsichord were plucked mechanically by a quill pick when the key was pressed down, so that it was not possible to vary the strength of individual notes. Additional keyboards, even a pedal manual, were added to try to overcome this deficiency, and music of that time employed trills and other embellishments to make some notes more prominent.

By the year 1700, Cristofori had changed all this. He used two strings for each note, and a set of leather-covered hammers to strike them. He also developed a key mechanism to control the force of the hammers so that they could be played softly *(piano)* or loudly *(forte)*, which is essential to practically all good music. The tone was light because of the small block-shaped hammers and low-tensioned strings. But Cristofori's historic first piano caused no excitement; everyone thought it was 'just a harpsichord with hammers'.

Later he worked out a greatly improved key mechanism, or piano action, as it is now called. The principles of this new action, highly developed since his time, are all used in today's

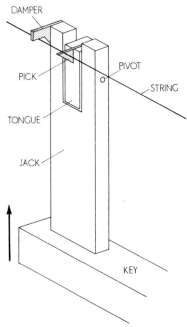

DAMPER

PICK

PIVOT

STRING

TONGUE

JACK

KEY

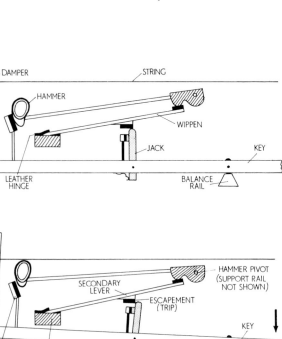

DAMPER

STRING

HAMMER

WIPPEN

JACK

KEY

LEATHER
HINGE

BALANCE
RAIL

SECONDARY
LEVER

HAMMER PIVOT
(SUPPORT RAIL
NOT SHOWN)

ESCAPEMENT
(TRIP)

KEY

BACK-
CHECK

LEVER HINGE
RAIL

BALANCE
RAIL

grand pianos, in spite of the fact that several less successful actions have been invented in the meantime. But Cristofori's work was to be forgotten for years; piano building later began again in Germany.

Referring to Cristofori's first effort, one writer commented: 'It was a noisebox where one note drums, another rattles, another buzzes, killing every feeling with hammers' (see Rene Clemenicic, *Old Musical Instruments*). Obviously the tone of the first pianos was not as good as that of the highly developed harpsichords of the time. It took many years and the work of many inventors to bring the piano to its present state. Major contributions were made by piano builders in Germany, France, England, and the USA.

As well as changes in piano actions over the years, there was a gradual improvement of the wire strings. These were first made from brass, then soft iron; later cast-steel strings were introduced by Webster & Horsfall of Birmingham, England. Finally, there came the cold-drawn, high-tensile steel of today's tremendously strong and uniform piano wire.

The early pianos had wooden frames which had to be strengthened as stronger strings were pulled tighter. Iron bars were used at first. Finally the full cast-iron frame was added to the already heavy wooden frame. Together they withstand the 20-ton pull of the 230 or so strings in the modern grand piano. This great stress would have buckled and broken the first pianos.

(*opposite*)
Fig 1 Harpsichord key, jack and plectrum. In this diagram the original quill pick (plectrum) has been replaced by a triangular piece of hard leather. The drawing exaggerates the size of the pick; only its tip engages the string. There is a hog-bristle spring at the back of the tongue, and the lower end of the tongue and the slot in which it fits are bevelled so that the pick cannot swing forward. When the key is pressed down the damper is raised off the string and the pick plucks the string. The tongue swings back, and as the key is released the hog-bristle spring returns the tongue to its original rest position.

Fig 2 Sketch of Cristofori's first piano action, apparently included in an inventory of instruments belonging to Ferdinando de Medici, dated 1700 (see Rene Clemenicic, *Old Musical Instruments*)

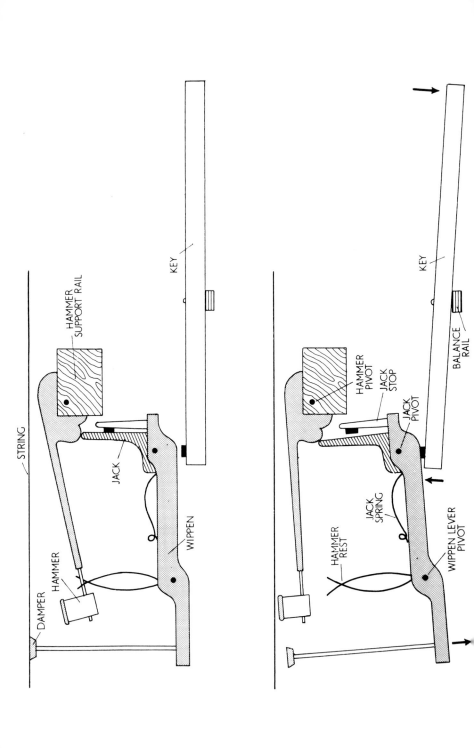

STRING

HAMMER SUPPORT RAIL

KEY

DAMPER

HAMMER

JACK

WIPPEN

HAMMER PIVOT

JACK STOP

JACK PIVOT

BALANCE RAIL

KEY

HAMMER REST

JACK SPRING

WIPPEN LEVER PIVOT

Today all pianos have iron frames, and are so similar in all important details that pianists have no difficulty in playing them wherever they are made, be it Japan, China, Germany, England, the USA or elsewhere. Piano tuner-technicians also find no difficulty in tuning and regulating them.

Pianos today are ruggedly made, strong in some ways but delicate in others. For instance, on one occasion a large upright was being taken in through a third-floor window when the hoisting rope broke, and the piano landed on its rear corner on the pavement below. Two tuners were called in to assess the damage. The wood was crushed on one corner, but there was no other damage and the piano was hardly out of tune. On the other hand, it is not unknown for the front to pull away from the back of a piano while it is simply sitting in the house. The causes of this kind of problem are discussed later.

There is also a saying in the piano trade that 'no one is expert unless he has broken the top hammer of a grand'. Sliding the action out of a grand piano requires a slight pull and it is difficult to avoid touching the end keys because of the width of the key frame. The hammer moves up, catches on the low pin-plank, and a light tug breaks the hammer. The action is delicate if improperly treated; even when dusting the inside of an upright piano it is easy to dislodge the hammer or damper strings.

(*opposite*)
Fig 3   Cristofori double-lever action, 1720. This and the previous figure are based on copies of drawings made by Marchese Maffei during his visits to Florence about 1709 and 1720. The escapement arrangement shown here has been simplified for clarity.

In Cristofori's first piano action the jack worked directly on the hammer butt. In this later action the jack raises the added intermediate lever, which in turn pushes the hammer up to the strings. The jack is arranged so that it slips off the pad on the lever before the hammer can jam against the strings. The added back-check prevents the hammer from rebounding and striking the strings more than once (blubbering), and also sets the distance of the hammer from the strings. The introduction of the second lever gives faster acceleration to the hammer.

2 Buying a Piano

Who can help you choose a piano? Sometimes the music teacher can, but many teachers have little or no experience in judging pianos and are put in an awkward position when they are expected to be experts. In most cases, if you must have help, the independent tuner–technician is likely to be your best man, as he tunes and repairs up to a thousand pianos a year. No one else tries out so many different makes under so many different conditions, or is more aware of how good or bad they are.

The well-established, reputable dealer knows more about prices and values, as that is his field. He can be relied on to help the buyer choose, especially among his own stock of instruments. The dealer should have a competent repair staff, and be authorised by the factory to repair any piano which comes under their guarantee. The piano guarantee usually states that if you send the piano back to the factory, they will repair it free of charge; but since the factory may be in East Germany, or Japan, or the USA, this is of little help, as you will be required to pay for freight charges.

Buying a piano by name has some points in its favour, but care should be taken as many well-known makers have been taken over by other manufacturers (see Appendix I). As a result some well-known piano names cannot be relied on as they once were.

A number of makers point to exclusive technical features in their pianos, indicating that other makes cannot be as good. This is not necessarily true. The exclusive feature may improve the tone of that particular piano but might not be an improvement in another make. The criterion must always be good tone rather than the maker's claims to special features.

When buying a used piano remember that the serial number stamped on the plate, the pin-plank, or sometimes on the soundboard will indicate the year of manufacture. Age is not the only factor to consider, but it is sometimes a useful guide; *Pierce's Piano Atlas* lists the makes, serial numbers and years of many pianos.

Do not rely on what you remember of the fine old instrument you had as a child. Pianos do not improve with age: the hammers become worn and the strings stiff, if not rusted; the soundboard may collapse (lose its crown), or crack; bridges and tuning pins become loose. Let's face it, pianos can become old and worn out, and sound that way. But people get used to their own piano, and automatically compensate for its defects when listening or playing. They even get used to its being out of tune, sometimes for years, and don't like it when it is finally tuned.

There are a few old upright pianos which have managed to retain a good deal of their original tone and have not been worn out with playing. Unfortunately, the best pianos are usually bought by musicians, who of course give them more work than the ordinary piano gets, so that a good used piano, especially one with a good name, is hard to find.

Many of these older pianos can be reconditioned in a good workshop and brought back to reasonable playing shape. It is better to buy a reconditioned piano than one which you plan to have overhauled. It is quite possible to spend a lot of money on reconditioning an instrument only to find that it is still unsatisfactory.

As a guideline when buying a piano, old or new, keep in mind the following rules.

Rules for Buying a Piano

1 Start by comparing pianos at every opportunity. Compare the good with the bad, the old with the new. Don't use recordings.

2 Establish the main use of the piano. Is it for concert work, teaching, school or other institution, playing at home,

or beginner's practice? The concert pianist requires a good grand to display his abilities, while a small console would be suitable for a beginner. The studio-type piano or the new full-size upright is usually suitable for schools.

Have in mind suitable appearance; the piano should look right. The element of prestige may be important.

3   Compare the room in which the piano is being appraised with the room in which it will be played. Will it be played in a ringy resonant room, or in an elegant and quiet drawing-room? Should the tone of the piano be brilliant, or more rounded and smooth?

4   Buy by tone and action. Look for musical quality, and a fast standard weight of action (see chapters 3 and 6). Avoid the strident and brassy, and the too soft and mushy tone. Compare the tone with that of a good new grand piano if possible. The tone should be clear, and even all across the instrument, with no abrupt change in tone at the break between bass and treble. The tone should have a musical sound, and please the ear of the buyer.

The piano should be up to pitch (standard A440) to give the best tone. It should also be in tune so that the average person when judging tone will not be confused by the twanging sound of an out-of-tune piano. Avoid pianos with a 'honky-tonk' or tinny sound.

5   Buy as new a piano as you can afford; old pianos are not better than new ones if they are of the same type. Don't just buy a big old piano, even if it has been reconditioned. Listen carefully to the tone. Test it thoroughly. Have an independent technician check it for you.

6   Pianos with a well-known name will be expensive if the quality has been kept up. Do not rely on the manufacturer's advertising: even the worst piano has to be advertised and sold.

Remember that pianos with a stencil name (as distinct from a model name) are always second- or third-grade pianos. A stencil name is a trademark name, other than the firm's own name, which is used on their cheaper line of pianos. Sometimes a firm will buy and trademark the name of a defunct company and use it as a stencil name, and large retailers may buy a number of pianos and put their own trade name on them.

As distinct from this, some makers use names for their various models – Liszt, Bach, Sherwood, etc – and put them on the front of the piano, with their own name inside. Always look for the manufacturer's own name, either on the front of the piano or inside on the iron plate.

7 Don't become involved in technicalities. What may appear to be poor design or construction may be the very opposite. If the piano is poorly designed or badly made it will show up in the tone or action. If the tone is not good, don't buy it.

A 'muffler' (quiet play) in a piano should seldom be used, and may not be necessary.

8 Buy a grand in preference to an upright, if you have room and can afford it. Stay away from pianos which are very small. This applies to both grands and uprights.

Don't be confused about 'upright grands'. There is no such piano, in spite of the fact that many big uprights have 'Cabinet Grand' or 'Upright Grand' on the nameboard, and people think they have something special. At one time upright pianos had two strings to each note and grands had three. Any piano which had three strings was a 'grand', but today all pianos have three strings to each note throughout the treble.

For comparison, the general sizes of pianos are as follows:

Upright pianos	Height of model
spinet	36–38in (91.4–96.5cm)
console	38–42in (96.5–106.7cm)
studio	45in (114.3cm)
full upright	48–51in (121.9–129.5cm)
old upright	50–58in (127.0–147.3cm)

Spinet and console pianos come in many different styles and finishes, many more than are available for grands or studio pianos. There is more emphasis on appearance than there is on tone.

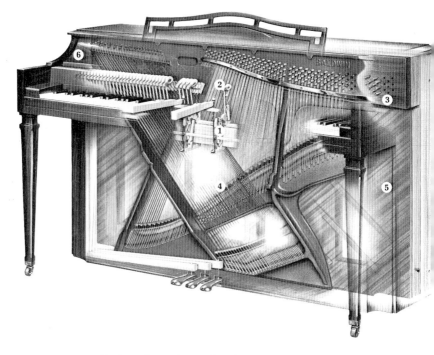

1   The Baldwin spinet piano, showing:
(1) The indirect action, which is placed behind and below the level of the piano keys, instead of above the ends of the keys as in the larger direct-action pianos.
(2) The position of the hammers and dampers, with the stringing indicated.
(3) The wooden pin-plank at the right, and the tuning pins which are driven into the pre-drilled holes. The iron plate (frame) overlaps the pin-plank. The stress of the strings is taken by the hitch-pins which are set in the lower part of the iron frame, and by the tuning pins in the pin-plank. The bottom edge of the pin-plank rests on a ledge cast on the back of the iron plate, thus transferring the total string stress of some 14 tons to the iron frame. The iron frame is supported and held rigid by the heavy wooden frame just seen at the back of the piano.
(4) The treble bridge extending across the soundboard, with the shorter bass bridge below.
(5) The spruce soundboard, with the grain and joints running in one direction and the ribs at right angles to them.
(6) The cabinet.
Courtesy of The Baldwin Piano Company, USA.

Grand pianos	Length of model
small grand	5ft (152.4cm) or 5ft 6in (167.6cm)
medium grand	6ft (182.9cm) or 6ft 6in (198.1cm)
large grand	7ft 6in (228.6cm)
concert grand	9ft (274.3cm)

The term 'baby grand' is seldom used by people who know pianos as it only indicates a small grand. Grands come in many sizes varying by only a few inches, from 4ft 6in (137.2cm) up, but the above are the basic sizes of grand pianos. They are measured full-length, from the edge of the lid at the back to the line of the key slip in front of the keys. A grand piano 5ft (152.4cm) in length is considered to be the smallest that a musician should buy, as he can do just as well tonally with a good upright.

When buying a grand it is sometimes useful to have the dealer make a paper pattern using a few strips of wrapping paper taped together. This is placed on top of the piano and the shape cut out with scissors. Placed on the floor, the pattern gives some idea of how much room the piano will take up, and perhaps where it will look best.

Appraising Used Pianos

When the qualified piano appraiser examines a used piano he adopts a procedure similar to the one outlined below, and makes a note of each detail. This prevents any oversight, makes evaluation easier, and can be retained for reference. More detailed explanation is given in later chapters.

External condition
1   Measure height of piano from floor. This establishes the type of piano: spinet, console, studio, or old upright. If it is a grand piano, the overall length is measured.
2   Note name of maker. A famous name adds value if the piano is good or can be restored. On the other hand, the name may detract from its value.
3   Check city or country of origin. If the piano is from a damp or hot, humid country and is going into a dry place, it

may be a questionable buy at any price, though there are exceptions: most new pianos use moisture-resistant glues, and the wood is treated to resist moisture.

4   Note style and colour. 'Louis' or 'French Provincial' are styles which tend to add value today, whereas heavier styles such as 'Empire' are not so much in demand. If the piano has antique value, describe it.

5   Check serial number. The make and serial number can be looked up in a book such as *Pierce's Piano Atlas* to find out the year of manufacture.

2   Console-type piano, 42in (106.7cm) high. Courtesy of Kawai Piano Co.

6 Examine bench. Does it match? Is it damaged?
7 Note condition of finish. Is it checked or scuffed? Will the piano require re-finishing?
8 Note condition of keys, ivory or plastic. These may need re-covering.
9 Note condition of castors and pedals. Will they have to be replaced?
10 Look out for the effects of damp, which can cause the bottoms of the back posts, and the castor blocks, to become loose.
11 Examine the iron frame. Is it full-size or three-quarter-size? Are there any cracks?

Internal condition
1 Test the whole piano for tone. Is the bass 'tubby', or the treble thin and weak? New sets of strings may be needed.
2 Examine condition of hammers. Is a full new set required, or will sanding restore them? Will replacing the top seven or fifteen suffice?
3 Test the tuning pins. If they are loose, an over-size set may need to be installed.
4 Check the action for wear. Is there side-play in the hammers or wippens? Should they be re-bushed, or do they only need the screws tightened?
5 Examine jack cushions, dampers, hammers and all felts under keys for moth damage. Replacement may be necessary.
6 Check condition of bridle straps. Are the leather tips dry and cracked? Have the tapes been eaten by mice? Will they require replacement?
7 Examine back-checks for wear. A full new set may be needed.
8 Check hammer and damper springs. These may be rusty and require replacement.
9 Check the key bushings. Turning the oval front-rail pins may take up the wear, but if badly worn they should be replaced.
10 Examine the soundboard from the front and back, for cracks, and to see if the ribs are loose.

3 Modern upright piano, 50in (127cm) high. Courtesy of Kawai Piano Co.

11 Examine bass and treble bridges. Note any loose bridge-pins, splitting between the pins, bridge laminations coming apart or looseness of the cap.

12 Examine along the joint of the pin-plank, back posts, and spacers at the top of the upright. If the front is pulling away from the back, this may appear as a fine crack anywhere along the joint, or the joint may be wide open, causing a drop in pitch.

An examination such as the above will indicate how much work must be done to restore the piano, and permit an estimate of cost to be made. The final chapters in this book

4 Medium or 'boudoir' grand piano,
6ft (182.9cm) long. Courtesy of
Welmar Pianos Ltd.

give a description of how the various repairs are done. The
appraiser can decide if the piano is worth reconditioning
fully, or whether a minimum of work should be done, or no
work at all. If the piano has to be taken to a workshop,
carriage costs must be added.

Many piano reconditioning jobs can be done in the home,
such as new felts under the keys, regulation of the action,
and minor repairs such as one or two new hammer shanks
which may have been broken.

5 Concert grand piano, 9ft (274.3cm) long. Courtesy of Welmar Pianos Ltd.

Action and key work usually requires that these parts be taken to the workshop. A new set of bridle straps, new jack cushions, new back-checks, etc, can be done in the home, but it is simpler in the shop.

Major repairs such as the back coming away from the front, re-stringing, new tuning pins, major soundboard work, new bridges, and re-finishing, all demand a workshop.

3 Judging Piano Tone

How to Tell Good Tone

The most important question when buying a piano is, 'How good is the tone?' The average person can learn to discriminate between good and bad tone quite quickly. All he needs is to know exactly what to look for, and some practice in comparing pianos.

In most reproductions of piano tone, as on records, tapes, television, etc, the tone is altered and is poor, especially in some sections, when compared to that of a first-class grand piano. Start, therefore, by comparing actual pianos – good and bad, old and new, grands and uprights. Practise listening to the piano, not the music, in homes, at concerts, in piano stores, or anywhere you can try out or listen to one. Imagine how it would sound in your own home. As you listen, ask yourself these questions:

Is the tone thin and hard (tinny), or too soft (mushy); or is it clear and sustained (a singing quality)?

Is the bass section dull (tubby); or is it resonant, clear, and deep?

Does the high treble sound like an extension of the centre section, as it should?

As a basis for understanding exactly what to look for, it should be made clear that each famous piano manufacturer has his own conception of good piano tone. The tone of each famous make is excellent, but there are differences; a pianist may therefore prefer one make of piano to another. Many people have read about the famous Canadian pianist Glen Gould going to Steinway's in New York and trying a number of pianos which they hold in readiness for concerts. He would pick a particular piano for one concert, then come back and choose another piano for a different programme of music. This is using an ability to judge the difference between excellent instruments to the best advantage.

For many years a number of the best concert pianists have been under contract to one manufacturer or another, to play only that make of piano in public. This is excellent advertising for the few manufacturers such as Steinway and Baldwin who persistently follow this policy, but tends to limit the public's exposure to other good instruments. On the other hand, the contract does assure the pianist and audience' of an excellent piano.

There are in fact differences between nearly all pianos, whether they come from one maker or from several. Where one pianist prefers a certain crisp clarity in the upper registers, another looks for a beautiful sympathetic tone, a special singing quality, not too bright and crisp. There are decided differences in the bass also, which will be discussed later, and the 'feel of the action' is very important to the pianist. When he finds an action he likes, he feels it gives him faultless and almost surprising control over the tone of the instrument.

'Buy a piano by tone and action': this is good advice, but how are good piano tone and good action to be judged? Some people buy by name, but while a Steinway or Bechstein or other great make of concert grands may be the best piano for a concert artist, it may be far too large, powerful and expensive for a person in a small apartment or home. It is obvious that the piano should suit the room both in size and tonal power. The concert grand has a powerful, clear, carrying tone, suitable for the recital or concert hall; but a piano for the home should perhaps be more suave and fitting, and should not dominate.

A piano that suits one room may not suit another. Some rooms have wall-to-wall carpeting, heavy drapes and over-stuffed furniture, and are quiet and absorbent. Others may have hardwood floors, thin drapes and furniture without upholstery, making them 'ringy' and resonant. Occasionally people find that even a small upright is too loud for their apartment, and demand a muffler or felt strip which is placed between the hammers and the strings. This, however, not only muffles the tone, but alters the action, and tends to create bad habits when the player endeavours to compensate for these changes.

Of course, power is only one aspect of good tone. The modern physicist can show in a drawing the various forms of vibration, and the differences in the pattern made by harmonics and overtones, which contribute to good piano tone, although this does not help one to choose an actual instrument. There are other complex factors which affect the tone of an instrument, including the size and shape, and the hardness or softness, of the soundboard; the number and placement of the ribs; the position of the bridges; and the down-bearing of the strings. The manufacturer has to contend with all these and more, but the player is interested only in the end result.

To be practical, let us examine some of the factors contributing to bad as opposed to good tone. Steel strings, for example, which have become 'stretch-hardened' or 'work-hardened' with age, lose their flexibility and elasticity. They become stiff and unresponsive, so that at least part of the piano is dull, instead of having a sustained singing tone. The bass strings may rust or corrode between the windings, so that they can be held out like a rod instead of a lively flexible string. This deterioration of strings is gradual, but may become so bad that the effect is similar to that obtained by playing while the hand is held against the strings. Try this, and also try a piano with a muffler. These are types of poor tone – the one muffled, the other dead.

When we come to discuss strings and the stringing of pianos (see chapter 14) we shall find that the bass strings are weighted with a copper winding to compensate for their being shortened. The weight of the copper winding slows the rate of vibration, producing a lower note. If this is necessary for a large grand piano, it is easy to understand why the spinet or the console pianos, where the bass strings are very short, present almost insurmountable problems in good tone production.

The factors concerned in all strings are length, thickness (weight) and tension, all of which involve stiffness. Each manufacturer uses his own special string formula balancing out those factors in conjunction with the specifications of the piano itself. Treble strings are not wound but are graduated in diameter (thickness) from extreme treble to bass.

Making strings very short distorts good string formula so that most small pianos, grand or upright, have very poor tone in the last few bass notes, sounding indeterminate in tone and pitch. There are confused wave beats in these low notes as though the string were out of tune in itself, and the tone is anything but rich, clear and resonant. Higher up the bass, in a poor-quality piano, the tone takes on a hard, almost trumpet-like sound, or alternatively is soft and mushy, in strong contrast to the tenor and treble sections.

Moreover, there may be faulty strings in the piano even when new. The copper winding may be loose and give off a rattle or a high-pitched sound. Instructions for dealing with this are given in chapter 14.

Soundboard defects also cause problems. Without a suitable soundboard the strings by themselves could hardly be heard. If the soundboard is too small, or is made of laminated wood such as plywood, the tone of the instrument will probably be poor in one section or another. These of course are the designer's or manufacturer's problems; the player is concerned only with the end result.

A factor which may have a greater bearing on the quality of tone is the hardness or softness of the hammers. If you put thumb-tacks into the 'striking face' of piano hammers to get a honky-tonk effect, as some people do, the result is a novel sound which soon becomes tiresome and jading. The idea, of course, is to imitate a worn-out bar-room piano. (Incidentally, tacks pushed into the felt hammers break down the felt, and the tacks bounce out and fall between the strings, or lodge against the soundboard; the hammers are ruined and the tone is spoiled.) To produce honky-tonk records the piano hammers were professionally treated. We were still able to recognise the piano sound, but this was in fact another form of extremely bad tone.

In some small modern pianos and some grands, the hammers are treated chemically to harden them, so that they produce a bright, big sound. This, of course, is the manufacturer's concept of what the public wants – big sound out of a small instrument – and in fact it does suit many people. Others tend to shy away from this bright sound, as it verges on the strident and brassy rather than producing the long, sustained, slightly softer and more musical sound which they would prefer.

Hammers can also be too soft, and although the tone may be pleasant, the pianist feels that he has to work hard to get results. The piano lacks a certain clarity and liveliness, the kind of tone that comes between a hard, harsh sound and a too-soft, lacklustre sound. Look for these basic differences when you compare pianos.

Piano hammers tend to harden unevenly with playing, or with changes in the humidity of the atmosphere. Damp tends to make the felt swell and the tone soft, while dryness shrinks and hardens the felt, making the tone hard. In the factory, when the new hammers are installed in the piano action they are usually too hard. After tuning a few times the voicer goes over the hammers, 'surfacing' them, and pushing a set of special needles into the hammer shoulders to create an air cushion behind the striking face. He can feel where the felt is too hard, and is familiar with the different pianos and their hammers, generally voicing them when out of the piano.

Final tone regulation is done quite quickly when the action is replaced in the piano: the resulting tone is full and rich, rather than thin and hard, being even all across the instrument. A good tuner, experienced in voicing or tone regulation, can often do wonders in improving the tone and evenness of even a mediocre piano. Voicing should only be done by an expert, as it is so easy to ruin the tone; moreover, the piano owner may be used to the tone as it is, and may resent a change.

One of the problems facing the appraiser or the buyer is

that of listening to the piano's basic tone, which may be masked by the instrument's being out of tune or having hammers which are not properly 'tone-regulated'. With practice this can be done, but only a technician can tell whether the poor tone is the result of, say, soft hammers, stiff strings or a collapsed soundboard. However, it is not difficult for anyone to recognise a piano with poor tone when comparing it directly with one which has good tone.

A neglected piano usually drops in pitch, which contributes to loss of tone quality. Raising the pitch say half a tone to the standard A440 (see chapter 8) can, of itself, produce a dramatic improvement in the tone of most pianos. But it goes without saying that it helps both buyer and seller if the piano has been tuned and voiced.

It must be emphasised that true judgement of piano tone comes from comparison between pianos, large and small, good and bad. The tone should be even right across the instrument, with no abrupt change in quality between one section and another, especially between the bass and treble sections. Treble and bass should merge smoothly at the 'break', which is where the stringing and the action itself are divided. The centre or tenor section of a piano is usually the best part, so special attention should be paid to the bass and the upper treble sections. The treble should sound like an extension of the centre section, neither harsh and brittle, nor soft and dull.

Look for any dull sections, or sections with a short and hard 'dinner-plate' tone. Look also for tone which disappears in the top octave, giving way to the knocking noise of the hammers. This may be due to the top hammers not striking the all-important correct striking point, or to too much felt on the top hammers blocking out the tone.

The expert appraiser particularly notes the bass section. Perhaps this is because a piano with a good bass is more likely to be good all across the instrument. As mentioned before, if the piano, whether grand or upright, is too small, the last few notes in the bass will be tubby. Compare them one at a time with the notes an octave higher, and if possible with any larger piano available. The bass should have a clear, resonant, full sound, from the bass break down to the end.

As the public becomes more aware of this general limitation of tone due to reduction of size, and manufacturers design more attractive cabinets for larger pianos with better tone, it is quite possible that a revival in sales of larger instruments will take place. Even as this is being written several makers are producing upright pianos 51in (129.5cm) high, which is the height of the old upright.

Cabinets have not yet been greatly improved in design, but this seems likely to come about as part of the continuing change in pianos. Small instruments are now available in bright colours, and a few grands were produced recently in beautiful soft shades of red, green and pale blue. The latter did not prove popular and have been withdrawn, but at the time they did seem to offer a new dimension to the interior decorator's art.

In conclusion, there are of course a number of factors which, although separate from the tone of the piano, do affect the final sound. For instance, the felt of the dampers may become wet from condensation on the strings. When a piano is shipped in very cold weather and brought into a warm room, moisture in the warm air condenses on the cold iron plate and strings so that water runs down the strings on to the dampers. When they dry and become hard, they make a pinging sound immediately the key is released, giving a wiry effect to the tone.

There are many objects in a room or on the piano which will vibrate in sympathy with certain notes, sounding like noises in the piano itself. Every tuner can tell stories about this 'sympathetic vibration'. For instance, a cup in a china cabinet, not sitting properly in its saucer, might vibrate when a certain note was played. The cabinet could be across the room, but the sound would appear to come from the piano.

In a more surprising case, the tuner had to ask to go down to the furnace room, where an overhead beam was found to have a long splinter which vibrated just below the piano. It would only vibrate when the automatic furnace went on and the heat affected it. Unfortunately the tuner called three times

when the furnace had shut off, and the owner of the piano
thought he was deaf. Eventually he arrived when the furnace
was on and was able to trace the sound.

How Tone is Made Up

For a broader understanding of piano tone the reader should
be reminded of how it is made up. When a piano string is set
in motion by the hammer, the full length of the string vibrates.
This produces what is called the 'fundamental' or 'prime'
tone – the lowest note of which that particular string is
capable.

We say the lowest note because at once each half of the
string begins to vibrate separately. The two halves vibrate at
twice the rate of the prime note, producing notes one octave
higher; these are called harmonics. The vibration of the string
immediately breaks up again into three parts, each sounding
an octave and a fifth above the lowest note. These in turn
break up again and physicists tell us that the string breaks up
into twenty or more partials, some of which are more
prominent than others. The less prominent harmonics are
called overtones.

Every musical instrument produces notes or vibrations,
each with its own particular set of harmonics. That is how
we are able to distinguish between a trumpet, a violin and a
piano, even when each plays the same note. The cello player
is one musician who can actually see the strings of his instrument vibrate, wholly and in segments, producing the fundamental note and its harmonics.

If a string or an instrument vibrates at 440 vibrations per
second, we hear this as the note A above middle C on the
piano. This A at standard pitch is referred to as A440. The
lowest note on the piano vibrates at 27.5 cycles per second,
and the top note at 4,186cps. In other words, the rate of
vibration establishes the pitch, and the number and intensity
of the harmonics establish the kind of tone and its quality.

Within the pattern of harmonics of the piano strings there
are slight variations. One piano may produce a note with

more prominent upper harmonics, and the tone will be harsh and hard. If the hammers are too soft, the strings will not vibrate as strongly, and the pattern or intensity of the harmonics changes, producing a soft or even a dull tone.

Many harmonics are out of tune with the fundamental note, some more so than others; the out-of-tuneness of these smaller harmonic sounds intrigues the ear, making the tone bright and lively rather than tame and uninteresting. A mixture stop on the pipe organ can be made of two or three ranks of pipes deliberately put slightly out of tune. The mixture is not used as a solo stop as it is too rough, but it does add liveliness to the full organ.

Piano manufacturers place the point at which the hammer strikes the string at one-sixth to one-ninth of its length from the top end. The hammer then strikes, and smothers the most offensive of the out-of-tune harmonics, thus improving the quality of tone.

4 Maintaining a New Piano

The new piano is usually tuned, and the action and finish checked over, before delivery. However, within about three months the piano should be tuned again, and then every four to six months for at least two years, depending on how heavily the instrument is played.

This regular tuning keeps the piano up to pitch, and gets some of the stretch out of the new strings. The new springy soundboard also settles down to a large extent, and the tuning pins in the pin-plank get fairly well set. Consequently the piano will stay much better in tune with the usual once-a-year tuning during the rest of its life. If, however, the piano gets a lot of heavy work, it must be tuned more often.

Earlier in this century pianos passed through the factory more slowly; the manufacturing pace was slower and the finishing or polishing of the case took longer. It took considerable time to dry and rub down a coat of shellac and seven coats of varnish, compared to spraying on a couple of coats of fast-drying lacquer. During this longer period in the factory, the piano was tuned as many as twelve times; by the time it was sold and delivered, it had settled down quite well, and would stay in tune for a reasonable time. Some factories now use a mechanical 'playing-in' machine which plays all the keys many times and settles the piano very well in a short time. But generally speaking the settling process today takes place mainly in the home, so that the buyer is responsible for the more frequent tunings required during the first two or three years.

Regulation of the action is not always required and not always done when a piano is tuned. However, the felts in the new piano gradually settle, and minor adjustments such as eliminating 'lost motion' between the keys and the action may be necessary. (Further regulation is discussed in chapter 5, and in greater detail in chapters 12 and 13.) The piano owner should ask the tuner to check the regulation, and adjust the pedals if necessary, so that the piano performs at its best.

One of the most important factors in caring for a piano, old or new, is placing it in the right atmosphere. Extremes of heat, cold, damp and dryness should be avoided if the instrument is to remain in good condition. Although the soundboard, the pin-plank, the ribs and the bridges are made of seasoned and kiln-dried wood, and are coated today with a moisture-proofing material, continual damp will finally make the wood swell, and continued dry heat will shrink it.

The instrument should not be placed where heat from the room heating system is directed at it. Steam from the kitchen, or damp from a window which is always open, may cause problems. Serious trouble can develop if a piano is kept in a damp basement, and minor basement flooding can be disastrous.

In extreme cases real problems begin when the piano is moved from a damp to a dry place. The wood dries and shrinks, and the glue tends to perish. The soundboard may warp and split, laminated bridges may separate and the ribs come loose. Even the spacing blocks between the tops of the back posts can loosen, and the pin-plank may shrink, leaving the tuning pins so loose that the piano will not stay in tune. These are all major defects which do not come under the manufacturer's guarantee because the piano has not been kept under satisfactory conditions.

Any experienced piano technician can tell whether or not the instrument has been kept under proper conditions – and often it is obvious to the non-expert as well. Water from a flower vase, or alcohol, may have been spilled into or on the piano. Pins, coins, pencils, toys, mouse nests, moths and so on are quite commonly found inside. If small children have access to the piano, they may tap the keys with a stick and chip the edges of the ivory or plastic covers, while rough pianists can break hammers and even strings.

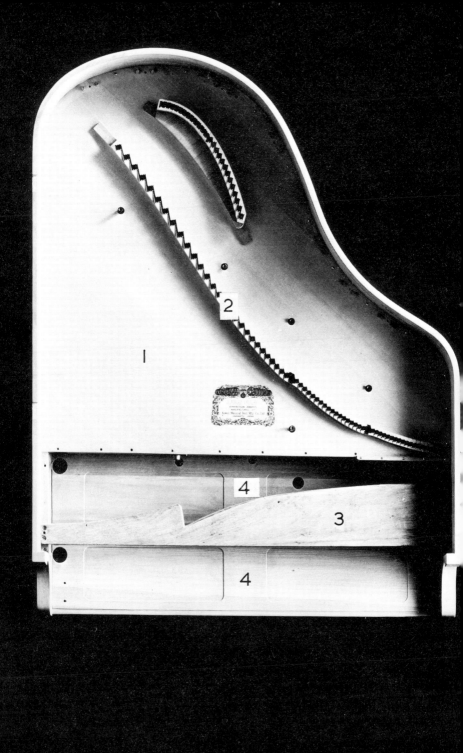

It is often said that a piano should not be placed against an outside wall. This idea probably stems from the fact that earlier houses were not insulated, and cold and damp could penetrate the walls. However, with modern warm and dry houses, an inside wall is not necessary for an upright. Some manufacturers still state that the piano should be placed on an inside wall, but they try to cover all possibilities, as their pianos may well go to remote places where conditions are not good.

Some years ago moths were one of the piano's main enemies. However, the moth-proofing now done by piano manufacturers is very effective, and moths do much less damage. In houses where they are still a problem, the piano technician should be asked to take out the keys and vacuum under them; keeping the felt punchings clean is one of the best preventatives.

With regard to the keys, whether plastic or ivory, all that is necessary to keep them clean is a damp cloth with perhaps a touch of mild soap. They should be rubbed with a dry cloth to restore their fine sheen. Abrasive cleaners and strong chemicals will ruin them, and should never be used. When the

6   Grand piano under construction. This photograph has been taken before the iron plate, strings or action have been installed. The spruce soundboard (1) is slightly convex; the long treble bridge (2) and the short bass bridge are glued and screwed to it. The edges of the soundboard rest on the lower, wider part of the rim (see plate 7).

The unusually shaped piece in front of the soundboard is the undrilled pin-plank (3). When the iron plate is put in position it fits closely over the pin-plank, and is bolted to it, as well as round the rim of the piano. Holes for the tuning pins are then drilled into the pin-plank, using holes pre-cast in the plate as guides. A lip on the underside of the plate fits down behind the pin-plank so that the plate itself takes most of the stress of the tightly pulled strings. A long opening in the plate between the soundboard and the pin-plank is bridged across, but allows the hammers to come up from below and strike the strings.

The damper unit is separate from the action and is positioned along the back of the key bed (4), so that the dampers themselves rest on the strings above the edge of the soundboard. The action is screwed on to the key frame after the keys are in position, and this whole action unit slides into place and rests on the key bed.

wood at the sides of the keys becomes soiled by the fingers, the keys should be taken out and the sides cleaned with a rag dampened with ammonia. Cloths used to clean the keys should be damp, not wet.

The sides of the keys should never be sandpapered. Sanding the sides widens the space between the keys, and taking off even a very small amount will spoil the neat, even appearance.

Piano cases used to be made of solid wood – rosewood, mahogany, walnut, etc. But the solid wood panels warped and cracked, and a core of white wood veneered on both sides eventually came to be used. This seldom warped, and the solid wood case went out of fashion about 1900. During 1960 compressed particle-board began to be used, and some expensive pianos now have this board veneered on both sides and on the edges for their case-work. Some types of particle-board withstand stress better than others, but it is a poor substitute for wood when made into piano benches.

Modern piano cases are usually finished with lacquer, although some manufacturers use a plastic finish, and a few still use varnish. A slightly dampened cloth will keep the dust off the lacquer and plastic, and a whiff of dust-remover sprayed on a cloth is all that is required to keep the dust off any finish.

7   View from beneath a grand piano under construction.
The rim (1) of the piano is built of laminations bent and glued into shape under pressure. The lower part of the rim is wider than the upper part, and heavy radiating supports or posts (2) complete this wooden frame. A ribbed soundboard (3) is fitted to the wooden frame, its edges resting on the wider part of the rim. A cast-iron frame is bolted to the rim above the soundboard, and the two frames together withstand the pull of some 230 strings, a total stress of up to 20 tons.
The soundboard is made of spruce and is slightly convex to withstand the downward pressure of the strings on the bridges. It is usually tapered toward the edges, and the ribs (4), also of spruce, have the ends shaved down to allow the soundboard more freedom to vibrate.
The pedal trap-work is fastened to the underside of the large key bed (5) and works through the holes provided. The front legs are fastened at the ends of the key bed. The support for the rear leg is not shown.

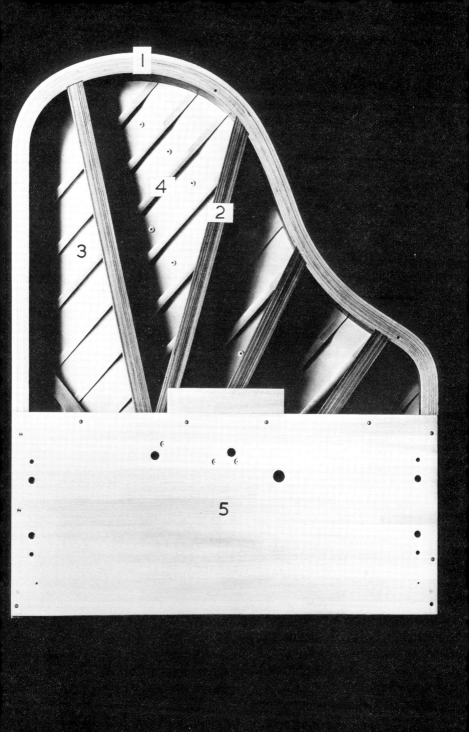

Polishes or waxes should be used sparingly. Most contain silicones, and there have been many instances where these have worked under the finish and turned it white. This necessitates stripping off the finish and re-finishing the affected part, and sometimes the whole piano. It is obvious that polishes containing silicones should be used only on occasion, and then sparingly; furniture re-finishing shops are well aware of this problem.

Care should be taken when dusting the action of the upright piano, as it is easy to dislodge the hammer springs or the damper springs. They operate in an open groove, and easily catch on the dust-cloth. Hammers, dampers and wippens cannot be moved sideways without breakage, so that careful dusting with a small brush and vacuum cleaner is probably the best method to use.

Dusting or cleaning the soundboard of a grand piano is always a problem. The best way is to take a tine from an old bamboo rake. Cut the bent end off and trim the straight piece so that it is slim and smooth. Use a slightly dampened rag to clean the soundboard at the back, where it can be got at. Then gently work the cloth under the strings with the bamboo, by putting it between the sets of strings and moving the cloth along gradually. The small bent bamboo piece can also be trimmed and used with the cloth for cleaning effectively under the top treble strings.

It is better to use bamboo than a flexible soundboard steel, as the inside of the lid or the band tends to get scratched unless you are experienced in using a steel. If water or drinks get spilled on to the soundboard, a similar method can be used to dry it up at once.

Pencils, pins or other small objects can be taken out with long tweezers, but if anything gets into the grand action, great care must be taken, as it is easy to break hammers when taking the action out or poking around in it.

Finally, if a piano is neglected, especially when nearly new, it gradually goes down in pitch. When the tuner finally pulls it up to pitch, it will not stay as well in tune as it would with ordinary care. So regular attention is important.

5 The Upright Action

The two main types of piano action now in use are the upright and the grand action. The old square piano action is obsolete, while the newer spinet action is a modification of the upright action. These actions fulfil a similar function, but they are different enough to require separate study. Upright pianos, the most popular, will be considered first.

The piano action is essentially a system of levers, the end of each lever moving in an arc when the piano is being played. The power and speed of the pianist's fingers are augmented by this system. His speed is increased five times, since the hammer moves five times farther than the key goes down: the key goes down $\frac{3}{8}$in (9.5mm), and the hammer moves $1\frac{7}{8}$in, equivalent to fifteen-eighths (47.6mm).

Each key has a complete action unit of its own, consisting of hammer, damper and wippen assemblies. There are eighty-eight keys and eighty-eight action units, which are made up in all of several thousand separate parts.

Nearly everyone knows that depressing the keys on the piano makes the hammers move forward and strike the strings. Fig 4 shows the piano key, which is kept in position by two guide-pins, one on the balance rail on which the key balances, and the other under the front end of the key. The front-rail pins are oval, and may be turned slightly to take up excessive wear or sideways movement of the key. The capstan screw near the back end of the key is adjustable, and contacts the action proper.

Fig 5 shows the hammer, which may have one or two layers of hard felt. The butt, or base of the hammer, is faced with felt pads and leather to cushion the upward thrusting action of the jack. The hammer is hinged by a wooden or plastic flange with a centre-pin which acts as a small axle. The centre-pin holes in the flange are bushed with red felt.

The second main moving part of the action, the wippen (fig 6), is not so well known. This short wooden lever is also hinged by a flange, and is raised by the capstan at the end of the key. In the upright action, the wippen is made to perform five different functions:

1   At the back end it carries the spoon which operates the damper.
2   It also carries the jack which lifts the hammer up to the strings.
3   It is a base for the jack spring, which pushes the jack back under the hammer butt when the key is released.
4   It carries the bridle wire to which the bridle strap is attached. The bridle strap ties the weight of the wippen to the hammer to speed up its return.
5   The wippen also carries the back-check, which catches and holds the returning hammer $\frac{5}{8}$in (15.9mm) from the strings. This allows quick, free return of the jack to its position under the hammer butt. It also prevents the hammer from 'blubbering' against the strings.

The third main moving part of the action is the damper lever (fig 7). It is hinged by a flange in the centre; the spoon on the wippen pushes out the lower end, so that the damper is lifted off the strings when the key is about halfway down. There is also a damper rod controlled by the sustaining pedal, which lifts all the dampers off the strings.

Fig 8 shows all the parts fastened in position on the main action rail, with the hammer spring, jack spring and damper spring in place. Although the working of the piano action is quite simple, it is an unfamiliar mechanism to most people, and a brief re-statement of how it works may be useful.

Depressing the key raises a small hinged lever called the wippen (see figs 4–8). The wippen carries a jack, which lifts the hammer in an arc, up and forward to the strings.

Before the hammer reaches the strings, the jack is tripped out of position, leaving the hammer free to strike the strings

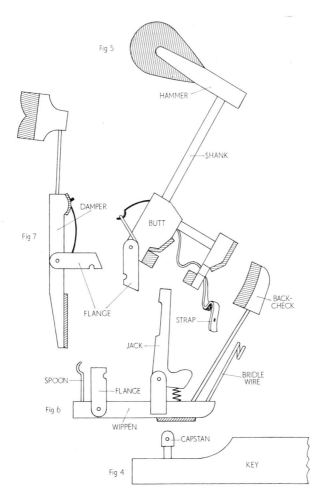

Figs 4–7 The upright action units: key (4), hammer (5), wippen (6) and damper (7).

and bounce back. On a held note the hammer is caught by the back-check, which prevents the hammer from 'blubbering', that is bouncing back and forth against the strings.

At the heel of the wippen is a damper spoon; this operates the damper lever, which lifts the damper from the strings when the key is halfway down.

When the key is released, the wippen drops, and the back check releases the hammer so that it returns to its resting place against the hammer rail. The jack slips back in place

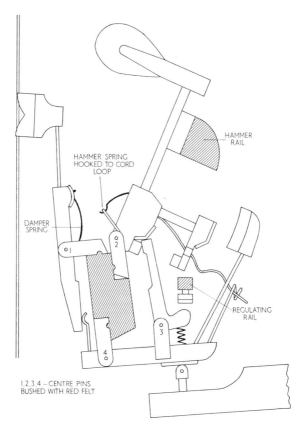

HAMMER
RAIL

HAMMER SPRING
HOOKED TO CORD
LOOP

DAMPER
SPRING

REGULATING
RAIL

1,2,3,4 — CENTRE PINS
BUSHED WITH RED FELT

Fig 8 The assembled upright action units.

immediately below the hammer butt. The return of the hammer is aided by the hammer spring, and by the bridle strap which ties the weight of the wippen to the returning hammer. The reaction of the damper lever spring pushing against the spoon also helps the wippen and therefore the hammer to return immediately to the normal position.

The return of all the action parts to position presses on the capstan screw at the end of the key, and this 'weight of action' causes the front end of the key to rise to its normal place.

The weight of action is so balanced against the weight of the key that an additional weight (finger pressure) of roughly 2–3oz (56.7–85g) will just make the note sound. This is referred to as the 'weight of touch'.

To make the action work properly it must be carefully regulated (adjusted), and each part must be regulated in correct order. The important points and the correct order of regulation are as follows, although regulation procedure goes much further when all the felts etc need to be replaced (see chapter 12).

1 *Hammer blow*   The standard hammer-rail setting, which controls the distance of the hammers from the strings, is usually $1\frac{7}{8}$in (47.6mm). Increasing the thickness of the pads which support the hammer rail will bring the hammers closer to the strings.

2 *Lost motion*   The capstan on the key must hold the wippen up far enough for the jack just to touch the hammer butt. If it is turned up too high, it will lift the hammers off the rail, and prevent the jack getting in and out freely from under the hammer butt. If the capstan is set too low, the key will go down slightly before the hammer starts to move. This is known as lost motion (slack) between the hammers and the keys.

3 *Levelling keys*   The keys must be level and at the correct height above the key bed, usually $2\frac{5}{8}$in (66.7mm). This should bring the top of the ivories $\frac{3}{4}$in (19.1mm) above the key slip (the thin wooden strip immediately in front of the keys), and about $\frac{1}{4}$in (6.4mm) below the height of the key blocks at each end of the keys. The general key height can be changed by unscrewing the balance rail and putting cardboard shims under it. Final levelling is done by putting paper punchings (washers) on the balance-rail pins under the keys.

4 *Depth of touch (key dip)*   Each key must go down $\frac{3}{8}$in (9.5mm), as measured over the front-rail pin, and this measurement is regulated by adding or removing paper punchings under the front-rail felt punchings.

5 *Trip (let-off)*   The jack must carry the hammer to within $\frac{1}{8}$in (3.2mm) to $\frac{1}{4}$in (6.4mm) from the strings before it trips out from under the hammer butt. If it trips too late the hammer will jam against the strings. If it trips too soon the note may miss playing altogether when played softly.

6 *Back-check* On a sustained note the back-check should catch the hammer $\frac{5}{8}$in (15.9mm) from the strings. This is adjusted by bending the back-check wire.

7 *Dampers* The damper should begin to lift when the key is about halfway down, and all the dampers must lift evenly when the loud (sustaining) pedal is used. Bend the damper wires first to make all the dampers lift evenly when the sustaining pedal is used. Bend the damper spoons (on the wippen) to make the damper lift when the key is halfway down. There are no dampers for the top octave and a half or so. The short duration of sound here makes damping unnecessary.

In spite of the foregoing, there are many pianos today which are designed to work with a hammer blow of $1\frac{3}{4}$in (44.5mm) instead of $1\frac{7}{8}$in (47.6mm) and a key dip $\frac{1}{16}$in (1.6mm) deeper than the standard $\frac{3}{8}$in (9.5mm). If you are not sure which figure to use, either write to the manufacturer for instructions or set one unit of the action at the usual figures and, if it does not work well, bring the hammers to within $1\frac{3}{4}$in (44.5mm) of the strings and increase the depth of touch to about $\frac{7}{16}$in (11.1mm) until the jack trips properly.

The pedal arrangement on the upright piano consists of two or three pedals. The sustaining or loud pedal lifts all the dampers off the strings. This allows each played note to continue sounding, and also permits other strings to vibrate in sympathy with it. It must be used judiciously to prevent a confusion of sound.

The soft pedal lifts the hammer rail and brings the hammers closer to the strings. The hammer 'travel' is thus shortened from $1\frac{7}{8}$in (47.6mm) to $1\frac{1}{8}$in (28.6mm). This shorter throw reduces the power of the hammer blow, and is most effective if the notes are played softly while the pedal is depressed.

A minor defect in upright pianos is that in using the soft pedal, lost motion or play is created between the keys and the hammers. In other words, the key goes down slightly, before the hammer moves, instead of the key and the hammer moving together. This occurs because the hammers are lifted closer to the strings and away from the top of the jack. Normally, the jack should just touch the base of the hammer butt when the action is at rest. Some upright actions were made to overcome this defect, but they were more complicated and are not now in use.

The centre pedal, which is more common in North American pianos than in European instruments, usually lifts the bass set of dampers only, and is referred to as a 'sustained bass'. On some makes the sustained bass is left out, being seldom used. Instead a muffler is attached to the centre pedal. This strip of felt moves down between the hammers and the strings when the pedal is depressed, muffling the sound. Some mufflers are made of such thick felt that the student tends to thump, thus losing, or never developing, any sensitive control over the keyboard. The point at which the hammers 'let off' (the trip) has to be increased slightly to accommodate the thick felt strip.

The mandolin or honky-tonk attachment is a modification by which a flexible leather or plastic strip replaces the felt muffler strip. The strip is fringed, and a brass paper clip is squeezed on to each section of the fringe with pliers. The sections are separated by cuts $\frac{1}{8}$in (3.2mm) wide, and each section is wide enough to cover the three-string unison. When the hammer strikes the metal-tipped fringe a metallic sound is given off.

Of course, there are a number of variations on the standard action as described above. When the upright piano was reduced in height from 56in (142.2cm) for many old uprights to 41in (104.1cm) for the console and only 36in (91.4 cm) for the spinet model, problems were created in reducing the action to make it fit. The limiting factors are the correct striking line on the strings for the hammers and the height of the key bed from the floor. The keys must be at a comfortable height for playing, and the key bed must also be high enough to allow the player to use the pedals.

It was a simple matter to reduce the old upright action in which the key pushed up a long wooden sticker or rod. The sticker was attached to the action wippen. To lower the

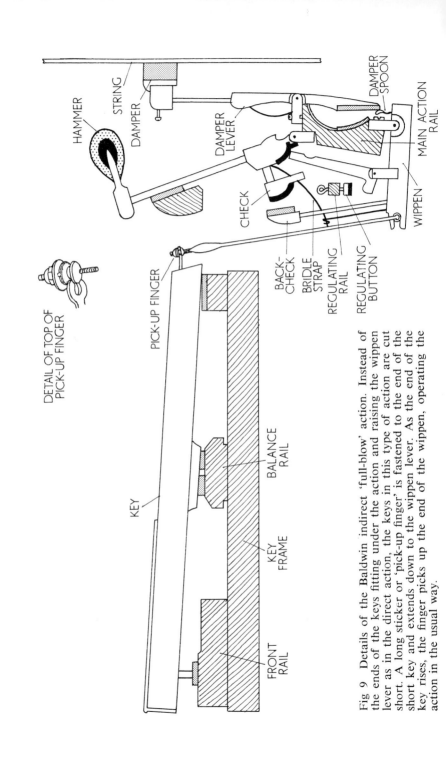

HAMMER

STRING

DAMPER

DAMPER LEVER

CHECK

DAMPER SPOON

MAIN ACTION RAIL

WIPPEN

BACK-CHECK

BRIDLE STRAP

REGULATING RAIL

REGULATING BUTTON

DETAIL OF TOP OF PICK-UP FINGER

PICK-UP FINGER

KEY

BALANCE RAIL

KEY FRAME

FRONT RAIL

Fig 9 Details of the Baldwin indirect 'full-blow' action. Instead of the ends of the keys fitting under the action and raising the wippen lever as in the direct action, the keys in this type of action are cut short. A long sticker or 'pick-up finger' is fastened to the end of the short key and extends down to the wippen lever. As the end of the key rises, the finger picks up the end of the wippen, operating the action in the usual way.

height of the action the sticker was done away with, and a shorter dowel arrangement, fastened to the key, took its place. This in turn was discarded in the console model, and a capstan screw at the end of the key came into contact directly with the wippen. The hammer shanks and other parts were also cut down in size. The key was shaved down at the rear to gain another half-inch, and the keys themselves tilted down toward the back to gain a little more height for the action.

The still smaller spinet model required a different approach as even the cut-down action of the console would not fit into it in the usual way. This problem was solved by cutting the keys off short and dropping the action down behind the short keys. A sticker was then attached to the key so that it reached down to the wippen and pulled it up, instead of the key pushing it up in the normal way. This indirect or drop action is not as satisfactory, or as easy to service, as a good direct action.

A variation of the direct blow action is made by Herrburger Brooks in England. The action appears to lie down in line with the keys, and is called a 90° inverted action; it works just like a standard action, in spite of its odd appearance.

The technician may also come across a Rippen piano, in which the tuning pins have a reverse thread and the sound-board a reverse crown. The hammer heel, not the shank, rests on the hammer rail. Details of different actions may be obtained from the makers or their agents.

In the old overdamper action, the damper lever and the damper itself are placed above the hammers instead of below them. The damper lever is lifted by a long vertical wire set in the front of the wippen, instead of by a damper spoon at the back end of the wippen. The series of long, evenly spaced, vertical wires along the front of the action gave rise to the name 'birdcage' action. The old overdamper has given way in the modern piano to the more positive underdamper action, although hundreds of thousands of the old-type actions were made, particularly in England, the birthplace of the mass-produced piano.

6 Good Piano Action

Any good piano action should be fast, quiet and responsive. The 'weight of touch' should be neither too light nor too heavy. The action of a new piano will not perform well if it is 'slow' or not properly regulated. A few pianos have poor balance arrangement between the 'weight of action' and the keys, which means that the keys do not return readily to their proper place.

Because of differences in construction, which are described in the next chapter, grand pianos do not have quite the same action problems as uprights. Although the same general principles apply, the remarks which follow apply chiefly to the upright mechanism.

Speed

A 'fast' action is one which should be capable of repeating a note faster than the pianist can play it; it depends basically on the keys. Testing to see if an action is fast can be done by trilling on two notes in different parts of the keyboard, or by the more expert method of drumming all the fingers one after another on one note. Use all the fingers of both hands if you can manage it.

Actions are often slow not through any fault in design of action and keys, but simply because of atmospheric conditions. High humidity, damp from an open window or damp basement, or steam from the kitchen, may make the wood around the bushings or the bushings themselves swell slightly. These tight felt bushings make some keys move slowly or even stay down. Such a condition is often temporary, but the sticking note always seems to be the one most needed.

In order to pinpoint the trouble in an unsatisfactory action, look first for slow or sticking keys. Hold a group of hammers against the strings and lift the keys up and down. They should be quite free. The piano technician can ease them if necessary with a pair of special key pliers, which compress the felt key bushings. Felt is used for the bushings as it makes the action quiet.

All the action bushings are very small when compared to the key bushings, and the centre-pin (about the diameter of a plain pin), which acts as a small axle, is very accurately fitted into its tiny bushings. They are fitted tightly enough to prevent side-play or wobble, yet not so tight as to impede the fast working of the action. Tight hammer bushings slow the hammers, while tight jack bushings will result in poor repetition, or may prevent the note from playing at all.

These small bushings can be eased with one of the new sprays which drive out moisture and lubricate the sticking part, or the felt can be shrunk with wood alcohol or with a mixture of alcohol and water, then dried thoroughly (see item 9, p. 122). This can be done only if the flange is made of wood, as alcohol can affect some plastic flanges and is not recommended for them. The centre-pin can be replaced, or a new flange complete with centre-pin may be fitted. As a rule, oil or water should not be used on a piano action.

If the keys are free, lift the hammers sufficiently to try the wippens. Tight wippen bushings will make the wippen and the key slow to respond. Hold a group of hammers against the strings and release them quickly, so that any slow hammer can then be seen. If the sustaining (loud) pedal is held down at the same time, any slowness will be accentuated, as the damper spring, being held off by the pedal, cannot assist the action to return to rest position.

In the upright, the jack is mounted on the wippen and can be seen behind the back-check wire and the bridle strap. When the key is depressed slowly the jack can be seen to trip on the regulation button, and fly out from under the hammer butt; the jack is sometimes referred to as the fly. When the key is released the jack returns to its place under the hammer butt. The regulation button controls the point at which the jack trips, and consequently the point at which the hammer breaks back from the strings. This is usually about $\frac{1}{4}-\frac{1}{8}$in (6.4–3.2mm) from the strings, allowing a little more in the bass than in the treble.

The capstan on the key controls the height of the jack. If it is set too high the jack cannot get back under the hammer butt, so the note will not repeat properly, if at all. The capstan may be set so high that it lifts the hammer off the hammer rail, which is quite wrong in the upright, although the grand action is built in just that way.

If the capstan on the upright action is set too low, there will be a space between the jack and the hammer butt. This results in lost motion, when the key goes down slightly before the hammer starts to move. Lost motion is easily seen by watching the back-checks while the keys are depressed slightly. The back-checks exaggerate the amount of lost motion because of their position, sticking up and out from the front end of the wippen (see fig 6).

The slow action may be due to a poor arrangement of balance between the weight of action and the keys. Piano keys are levers, and in small pianos particularly, the keys are short: the farther back the fulcrum point is placed (at the balance-rail pin), the heavier the action weight must be in order to lift the front end of the key to playing position.

In some poorly made small pianos both the hammer and the damper springs are strengthened for the sole purpose of making an otherwise slow action work reasonably quickly. Another method used to improve slow action is to insert lead weights into the extreme ends of the keys to make them return more quickly. Both methods make the weight of touch heavier. The latter is a rough variation of the factory method of balancing keys and action by inserting leads in the sides of the keys, at front or back, in order to give the correct graduated weight of touch from bass to treble.

Weight of touch is really the finger pressure required to make a note play, and pianos generally are regarded as having a light, medium or heavy touch. However, there are many different ways of playing a note – fast, slow, heavy or light, or using different fingers or thumb. There are also a number of mechanical factors which can complicate what appears to be a simple function.

Because of these variables, some makers use a 'down-travel weight' as a guide during assembly of the action and keys. A weight of about $1\frac{1}{2}$–2oz (42.5–56.7g) is placed on the front end of the key, which depresses the key slowly – so slowly in fact that the action frame must be thumped to make the weighted key creep down. It is not heavy enough to make the note play, and the jack does not quite escape from under the hammer butt. Even the damper is held off the strings by the pedal, and although this test may help the manufacturer it is not very useful to the pianist or the tuner–technician.

Measuring the weight of touch requires more than a static weight placed on the key. It will not be satisfactory unless the momentum of the finger is considered and the note actually sounds, indicating the completed movement of the action unit and key.

'Up-travel weight', on the other hand, is a measure of the weight of action. This is the combined pressure of the hammer spring, jack spring and damper spring, plus the gravity pull on the wippen and hammer. This combined pressure on the capstan lifts the front end of the key to position, and is much less than the pressure required to depress the key on the 'down travel'.

It will be realised that friction caused by any tight felt bushings in the action will impede the hammer in playing. This, of course, adds to the finger pressure or weight of touch necessary to play the note. Friction between the capstan and the wippen caused by corrosion or badly made capstans will also impede the hammers. Polishing the capstans and brushing the felt pad on the wippen will improve this. Unnecessary friction between the jack and the hammer butt can be reduced by smoothing and graphiting the top of the jack.

Such friction problems will contribute towards making a fast action slow. Another problem is lack of uniformity in the strength of the various springs in the upright action.

Hammer and damper springs can be improved by bending, but it may be necessary to take off the dampers to get at them.

The hammers are graduated in size from larger and heavier in the bass to the thinner and lighter hammers in the treble. The correct weight of touch should be just as evenly graduated. Inserting lead weights in the key to alter the weight of touch adds inertia, so that as little lead as possible is to be preferred.

Weight of touch means the actual weight required to make the note just sound, and no more. An adjustable weight can be placed on the front end of the key, and the key held up level with its neighbour. If the key is then released suddenly, the note should just sound.

The accepted average weight of touch across the keyboard is about $2\frac{1}{2}$oz (70.9g). A 2oz (56.7g) weight of touch is considered light, and a 3oz (85g) weight is heavy, although it is quite possible to find pianos with still heavier or lighter actions. Judging the weight of touch by hand, without a measuring device, can only be done through practice and comparison with other pianos. Even the experienced musician or technician can be confused sometimes, because of a certain smoothness, almost slickness, in certain individual pianos, while pianists' judgements of the same piano can vary considerably.

Although there is a manufactured adjustable weight available, it may be helpful to make up a simple weight composed of a short bolt and a number of washers. The correct weight of the bolt and the average weight of the washers should be established by using a druggist's apothecary scale, a post-office scale or other fine scales.

Make the weight up to, say, 2oz (56.7g) and place it on the front end of the key. Support the key with the tip of the finger at the correct level, then release it quickly. Add washers until the note can be heard faintly. Try this on all the keys, and calculate the average weight of touch. Ideally, the weight of touch should be graduated slightly from bass to treble, but do not be surprised if a few keys are not uniform.

If the action is only slightly uneven, it may not trouble the player at all, but if necessary the tuner–technician may be able to even it out by one means or another. He may, as already mentioned, be able to add or reduce weight. He may ease the bushings, or polish the capstan and brush the wippen felt. He may alter the position of the capstan, or the dowel if the action is of that type. Bringing the capstan forward makes it easier to lift the wippen and so lightens the weight of touch; placing the capstan farther back makes the touch correspondingly heavier.

If the keys and action are free, the technician may then insert the usual round leads into the side of the key, either toward the back or the front, or use a special long, flat lead which can be screwed on to the top of the key, if needed.

The ideal action would feel smooth and fast with a weight of touch of between $2\frac{1}{2}$oz (70.9g) and $2\frac{3}{4}$oz (78g), using the simple bolt and washer weight described above.

Quietness

The piano action should be quiet in operation. There should be no obvious sound from the keys and action parts during playing.

There is, of course, a certain amount of noise in any piano action, as it is a mechanism with many moving parts. If you concentrate on listening for these slight mechanical sounds, paying no attention to the music or to the tone of the instrument, it is quite possible to hear them.

Some people become very critical after buying a new piano, and listen only for defects. They begin to hear differences in the harmonics of individual notes, or the faint bumping of the keys and action parts. These slight differences and noises become more and more noticeable through continued concentration on them. This misdirected concentration sometimes results in the piano being sent back, and replaced by one in which the person cannot hear any defects at first.

Aside from the exaggerated attention to defects which are barely discernible to the professional pianist, there can be noises in the piano which no one is expected to disregard.

If the felt punchings under the front of the keys, or the bolster cloth under the back of the keys, are hard or too thin, the normal faint bumping may become loud enough to be objectionable. Sometimes the bolster cloth is tacked down instead of being glued, and the key may knock on a tack head. Too much glue can soak through cloth or felt, making keys or jacks rattle when it dries hard. Jack cushions (the felt squares on the hammer butts) may fall off because of lack of sufficient glue, and the jack then clacks against the unprotected hammer butt.

Hammer heads or back-checks may be loose, making knocking noises. Loose action screws may need to be tightened; indeed this is always the first item called for in regulating any action. Damper heads also can be loose, or the damper felt too compressed or hard, making 'zinging' noises which spoil the tone, despite the fact that the damper acts after the note has sounded.

The hammer-rail felt on which the hammer shanks rest is sometimes hard, and for a time foam rubber was used instead on some pianos. This perished, becoming hard and brittle, and had to be changed to ordinary felt because of the noise it made. Foam rubber was also used in place of bolster cloth under the ends of the keys, and again had to be replaced.

The pedals may squeak, and sympathetic vibration, which can cause anything loose, inside or outside the piano, to vibrate, may result in rattles and 'pinging' noises. The effect of sympathetic vibration can be very troublesome. There is such a wide variation in the rates of vibration between the extreme bass and the extreme treble strings that anything from a loose caster to the filament in a nearby lamp can rattle or vibrate in response to one note or another. Small objects, such as beads or broken ornaments, often fall down behind the piano and lodge against the soundboard; these will rattle when certain notes are played.

Serious defects, such as a cracked soundboard, a loose or poorly cut bridge, or loose copper windings on the bass strings, can cause noises which call for workshop repairs. The technician distinguishes between metal-to-metal sounds (as in the lock on the piano) or wood-to-wood sounds when trying to pinpoint the source of trouble.

Responsiveness

A good action is responsive. This is a difficult attribute to describe, although it is quite common for a pianist to praise a particular action.

The responsive action lends itself to the pianist's mood so that he can trill with a crescendo or diminuendo with ease and satisfaction, or make a theme or melody stand out clearly from block chords. In other words, the action offers good control. Combined with the right weight of touch, and with good tone, it entices the pianist to play for the sheer pleasure of playing. Responsiveness indicates a special 'feel' as well as good performance in an action.

An action is not responsive if it tends to miss playing when a note is played very softly; or if the hammer blubbers against the strings; or if one note is louder (the hammer being harder) than another. Any condition that prevents the pianist having complete control in executing subtle nuances, or accenting individual notes in chords or passages, would indicate an unresponsive action.

Apart from these obvious defects, which are due to lack of regulation (adjustment) of the action and tone, there are more subtle differences. As described previously, if the felts under the front of the keys (front-rail punchings) are too compressed or hard, they may be noisy: they will also contribute to hard playing. The pianist finds this lack of resilience tiring. There is a slight flexibility in a properly made piano key; together with the correct resilience in the felt punchings it contributes to the satisfactory feel of a responsive action. If friction between the capstan and the wippen, and between the jack and the hammer butt, is reduced to a minimum, this too can add greatly to the responsiveness of an instrument.

If the damper and hammer springs are too strong, the key may go down smoothly, but when the jack escapes with a jump, the pianist may feel a jerky, double-touch effect which tends to interfere with good control.

Where the hammer butt is contacted by the top of the jack, it is not only covered with soft buckskin, but if well made has two separate felt pads under the leather. In addition the butt is shaped to allow the jack to lift the hammer, and, as it goes up and forward, to allow the jack to slip out and in easily without sticking or jerking. Where the butt felt or leather is uneven or worn, this may be remedied by sewing a stitch or two of thick wool yarn through behind the leather.

If the manufacturer's dimensions are adhered to, there should be a certain amount of 'after-touch': that is, the jack should clear the hammer butt by about $\frac{3}{64}$in (1.2mm) when the key is held down. This ensures good clearance to allow the back-check to catch and hold the hammer, and adds greatly to the satisfactory feeling of a responsive action.

The back-checking should be correct and even and the bridle straps adjusted, and the dampers should begin to rise when the key is halfway down. The dampers must also rise evenly when the sustaining pedal is used, and the hammers must be tone-regulated. (These items are covered in more detail in chapter 12.)

In order to get a smooth feel with complete control of the action, it is sometimes necessary to change slightly the strict regulation measurements which are normally used.

7 The Grand Piano Action

The grand piano action is superior to the upright action. It is more complex and is based on Cristofori's concept of a double-lever action, whereas the upright has a single lever, the wippen, which as noted earlier has to perform as many as five separate functions.

Moreover, the horizontal position of the grand action allows the pianist positive control in raising the hammers to the strings and dispenses with springs as the hammers fall back to rest position. In contrast, the vertical position of the upright hammers requires the use of springs which vary in strength, and also the 'bridle-tape-to-wippen' arrangement to hasten the return of the hammers.

In the grand double-lever action, the damper mechanism is separate, being operated by the extreme end of the key, not by the action proper. When the grand action is removed, the entire damper and *sostenuto* mechanisms are left in the piano; each individual damper must be unscrewed and taken out before the rest of the damper action can be removed.

The wippen in the grand action embodies the double-lever system. It is more complex and more sophisticated than the single-lever wippen of the upright. The lower part or main body of the grand wippen is a lever in itself, and is raised by the capstan on the key in precisely the same way as on the upright. The grand wippen does not carry the back-check, as this is mounted on the key itself near the back end, nor does it carry a bridle wire as there are no bridle straps in the grand action. This lower or main part does carry the jack, and it also acts as a support for the upper or repetition lever.

The repetition lever supports the weight of the hammer, while the jack operates through a slot in the lever. In other

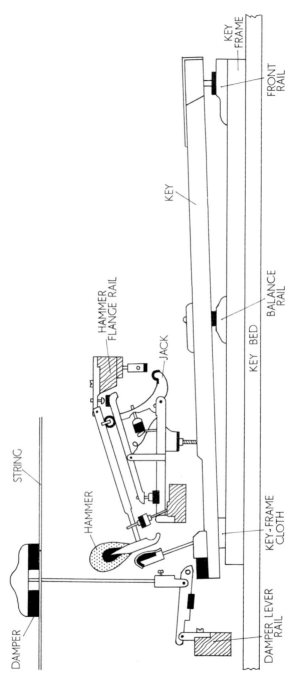

STRING

DAMPER

HAMMER

HAMMER FLANGE RAIL

JACK

KEY

KEY FRAME

FRONT RAIL

BALANCE RAIL

KEY BED

KEY-FRAME CLOTH

DAMPER LEVER RAIL

(*above*) Fig 10 Grand action and key. This drawing shows the grand piano action as made by Pratt-Read Piano Action Co, USA. Actions made by various manufacturers show minor differences: for instance, compare this drawing with plate 8. (*below*) Fig 11 Detail of the damper, wippen assembly and key in the grand action. Chapter 13 explains how to regulate the action to give maximum efficiency.

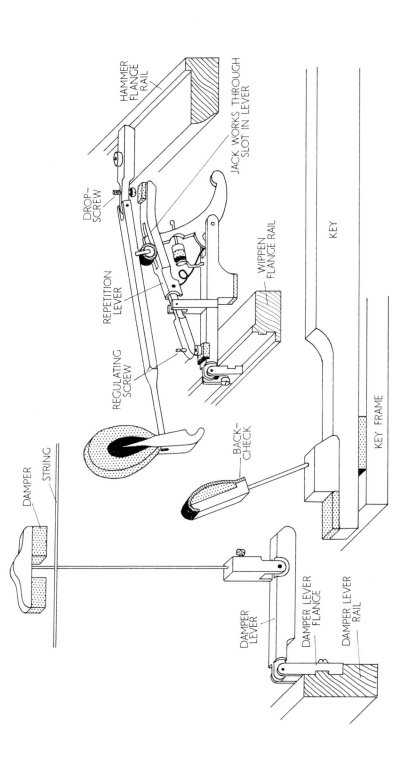

HAMMER FLANGE RAIL

JACK WORKS THROUGH SLOT IN LEVER

DROP-SCREW

REPETITION LEVER

WIPPEN FLANGE RAIL

KEY

REGULATING SCREW

DAMPER

STRING

BACK-CHECK

KEY FRAME

DAMPER LEVER

DAMPER LEVER FLANGE

DAMPER LEVER RAIL

8 Grand action at rest position. The back edge of the jack is in line with the back edge of the wooden core of the hammer roller. This is the correct position. Adjustment is made by the screw at the centre of the jack. The weight of the hammer is carried by the repetition lever, which should hold the hammer shank about $\frac{3}{16}$in (4.8mm) above the hammer rail or rest pad. Normally the point of the hammer head should be $1\frac{7}{8}$in (47.6mm) from the strings, but on this piano it is $1\frac{13}{16}$in (46mm). This Japanese Kawai grand action model does not include the *sostenuto* mechanism.

words, the roller or knuckle on the hammer shank lies across the slot in the repetition lever, while the jack rests almost through the slot, and just below the hammer roller. The hammer roller performs the same function as the hammer butt in the upright action. When played, the jack protrudes through the repetition lever, lifting the roller, and thus the hammer, up to the strings.

The jack is then tripped out from under the roller, and the hammer is caught on its return by the repetition lever. The lever is spring-loaded, and if the note is struck smartly and held, the lever gives way sufficiently to allow the heel of the hammer to be caught by the back-check. At this point, if the key is released slowly, the hammer should rise a little, as the spring in the repetition lever lifts the hammer clear of the back-check. This ingenious arrangement permits the jack to move out or in freely from under the hammer roller, and enables the pianist to trill with the keys halfway down.

The keys in the grand piano are several inches longer than the keys in the modern upright. The additional leverage provided in this way allows the designer more scope in balancing the weight of the action against the weight of the keys. The capstan, which lifts the wippen, can be placed at the very best position to lift the wippen mechanism; and the extreme end of the key provides leverage to lift the damper assembly without adding unnecessary weight to the touch.

The damper in the grand piano drops down on to the strings without the aid of springs. It is connected to a hinged, weighted damper lever, which makes the damping more positive and effective than in the upright action.

In the grand piano it is possible to place the dampers in the best position along the strings without interfering with the hammers. The hammers work on the opposite side of the strings, and the best damping position may be very close to the correct striking point for the hammers. The dampers clear the strings well before the hammer strikes.

The hammer and damper springs in the upright action may be too strong or too weak, or vary in strength, but this problem does not arise in the grand as there are no such springs. There are more adjustment (regulation) controls in the grand action which also contribute to its general efficiency.

The keys of all pianos, grand or upright, are arranged on a key frame. The frame has a back rail, a centre or balance rail, and a front rail. The key frame of the upright is fastened to the key bed; but the grand key frame is removable, and slides out, complete with keys and action in one unit.

The keys of the upright can be taken out while the action remains in place. The keys of the grand cannot be removed in the same way, as the grand action is screwed on to the key frame after the keys are placed in position. The back-checks on the grand are near the end of the keys, so that the keys cannot be drawn forward for removal without first unscrewing the action.

9 Grand action position on sustained note. The capstan on the key has raised the wippen, and the jack has lifted the hammer to $\frac{1}{16}$in (1.6mm) from the strings. The jack is then tripped out from under the hammer roller by the regulation button which is above the toe of the jack.

The hammer has bounced back from the strings and has been caught first by the repetition lever, then by the back-check at $\frac{5}{8}$in (15.9mm) from the strings. The damper lever is raised by the end of the key, and the damper is held off the strings, sustaining the note. This photograph demonstrates that the damper mechanism is separate from the piano action.

A major advantage in the grand piano is in the working of the soft pedal. When the soft pedal is used, the entire key frame carrying the keys, hammers and action is moved to one side. This sideways movement is small, but enough to make the hammers strike two strings instead of three, or one string instead of two in the upper bass section. This cuts down the volume of sound, but does not alter the action as the soft pedal does in the upright piano.

Cristofori invented the *una corda* arrangement which moved the hammers so that they struck only one string. His pianos had only two strings, so that the term *una corda* (one string) was correct. It is no longer correct to use this name for the soft pedal in a modern grand piano as most of the piano has three strings for each note. The pedal is sometimes referred to as the shift pedal, but soft pedal is the accepted term.

In a number of old grand pianos, the centre pedal lifted the bass set of dampers, and was usually called a 'sustained bass'.

This system is generally found in modern upright pianos, but in a good grand, equipped with three pedals, the centre pedal is a true *sostenuto*.

In using the *sostenuto*, the pedal must be depressed after the note or chord has been played, and while the keys are still held down. It will then sustain only the notes played. When the key is depressed, the damper is raised; the *sostenuto* pedal turns a rod which has a lip running its full length, and this lip engages a metal tab protruding from each damper, thus preventing the damper from returning to position and sustaining the particular note or chord played.

The *sostenuto* pedal can be used in several ways. For instance, if the loud (sustaining) pedal is held down, and then a chord is struck, the harmony of the chord becomes confused as it picks up harmonics from other strings by sympathetic vibration. However, if the chord is struck, then sustained by the *sostenuto* pedal, the harmony remains clear and beautiful.

The last note on a soft running chord can be caught and sustained alone, until it dies away, if the *sostenuto* pedal is used expertly. A note can be pre-selected, within limits, by putting the key down softly so that it does not sound, then holding it with the *sostenuto* pedal. It will then be sustained automatically next time the key is played. The beginner should be warned that if the *sostenuto* pedal is used improperly – that is, at the same time as the note is struck – it is quite possible to bend the metal tabs on the damper mechanism, making them useless.

The right-hand pedal in all pianos lifts the dampers off the strings, sustaining the tone. If the pedal 'trap-work', and the dampers themselves, are not adjusted properly, the dampers may not rise sufficiently or evenly. The pedal itself may go down too far for comfort, or it may not go down far enough, in which case it will feel blocked. The piano technician can easily remedy these problems.

The soft pedal should be adjusted so that the piano action and hammers move sideways far enough to clear one string. To test this, hold the soft pedal down, and at the same time block the two right-hand strings. When the note is played, none of the three strings should sound. The action 'shift' should be regulated so that the edges of the hammers do not strike the strings, as this will spoil the tone.

The correct height of the keys is set in the factory and varies slightly with each maker. It is usually about $2\frac{1}{2}$–$2\frac{5}{8}$in (63.5–66.7mm) from the key bed, and about $\frac{1}{4}$in (6.4mm) below the level of the end key blocks. The correct height must be comfortable for playing, and in one European piano (Bosendorfer, Vienna) is measured as $28\frac{1}{2}$in (72.5cm) from the floor. It contributes to the good appearance of the piano in that the keys are not too high above the key slip (the wooden strip in front of the keys). Keys that are too high look like false teeth, and if they are too low the pianist feels restricted, as his fingers almost touch the key slip. In some pianos the key slip is bevelled or curved to give a sense of freedom to the player.

The height of the key is controlled by two factors: first, by the thickness of the bolster cloth on which the back end of the key rests, and second, by the thickness of the balance-rail cloth punchings under the middle of the keys. The keys rest on these two points, and the slightest change at the balance rail makes a noticeable difference in the key level.

Bolster cloth or back-rail cloth, hammer-rail cloth and the punchings under the keys are basically baize, which is a coarse cloth napped to imitate felt. Sometimes these cloths are referred to as felts, even by some piano makers and supply houses, simply because they look like felt.

The keys must be level to give uniformity of action and good appearance. To level the keys, thin paper punchings are used under the balance-rail cloth punchings. Some of the paper punchings are thinner than cigarette paper.

The depth of touch is the distance the keys go down, and the measurement must be exact if the action is to perform well. The depth of touch is controlled by the thickness of the front-rail punchings – that is, the baize or cloth washers used under the front or playing end of the keys. Fine adjustments are made by using thin cardboard or paper front-rail punchings under the cloth punchings. Five different thicknesses of baize strip and five thicknesses of cloth punchings, in addition to about twenty-five thicknesses of paper punchings for both front rail and balance rail, are available to the trade. Different shades of colour are used to identify the different thicknesses of paper punching.

For a long time the depth of touch has been set at $\frac{3}{8}$in (9.5mm) for the grand piano. But there is a tendency for the so-called felts to settle or pack, which may result in a change in the depth of touch, particularly in the centre section of the piano where it is most heavily played. Some makers anticipate this and leave the depth of touch slightly deeper in this area.

If the back-rail or bolster cloth should settle or pack, this will not only affect the depth of touch, but will also allow the wippen to drop slightly. In the grand action the hammer is normally supported by the repetition lever, which is the upper part of the wippen. When the height of the wippen and the repetition lever is lowered the hammer also drops farther away from the strings, and the action loses efficiency.

In the upright action, when the wippen drops the jack comes away from the hammer butt. This causes lost motion (play) between the keys and the hammers. Turning up the capstan screw on the key of either action corrects the situation.

When a staccato note is struck, the returning hammer breaks through the resistance of the repetition lever spring and strikes the rest cushion (or hammer rail) before being brought back to its normal position, which is about $\frac{3}{16}$in (4.8mm) above the rest cushion. When a note is struck and held, the returning hammer overcomes the resistance of the lever spring, pushing the lever down until the hammer is caught by the back-check $\frac{5}{8}$in (15.9mm) from the strings. The spring in the repetition lever should be strong enough to raise the hammer to its normal position as soon as the key (and the back-check) are released.

The hammer is supported at its correct distance from the strings. This is usually $1\frac{7}{8}$in (47.6mm), but many grands today use a distance of $1\frac{3}{4}$in (44.5mm). Where possible the correct figure should be obtained from the manufacturer or his agent.

Although there are minor differences in most pianos, there are a few grands which have unusual features, such as the Bluthner grand which has four strings to each note in the treble instead of the usual three. The extra string sits above the ordinary three strings supported by a tall individual bridge. It is not struck by the hammer but is designed to vibrate in sympathy with its parent note, adding to the resonance of the piano. These extra strings in the lower treble are tuned an octave above their parent string, and in the upper treble are tuned in unison with it. The normal strings are tuned in the ordinary way, and the fourth string is plucked by hand when tuning it.

The Bosendorfer concert grand has a few extra keys added to the extreme bass which have a separate cover of their own. The normal eighty-eight-note keyboard can thus be extended by these few notes for special performances.

The lower ends of the treble strings in Steinway and some other grands are not muted with stringing braid or tape as are most pianos, but are left free to vibrate in sympathy. They are designed to produce notes which are harmonics of the speaking strings. Some have individual metal bridges (aliquot bars) or aliquot plates with a series of individual bridges, which are placed on the iron frame near the hitch-pins. The harmonic section can be tuned separately from the string itself by moving the aliquot bar.

Part Two
Piano Tuning and Repair

8 Practical Piano Tuning: Stage 1

The experienced tuner–technician acquires a number of special tools for tuning, repairing and regulating pianos, but the beginner will only need a few to start with. They can be bought from music or piano stores, through a friendly piano tuner, or from piano supply houses. A supply house catalogue is almost essential for full details of tools and equipment.

Basic Tuning Equipment

Tuning hammer
Rubber mutes with wire handles, for bass and treble notes
Temperament strip. This is a strip of felt used to mute two octaves at a time by pushing between the groups of strings with a screwdriver; commonly used for muting the temperament octave
Tuning forks C523.3 and C517

Basic Regulating Tools

Key dip-block, to measure correct depth of touch and distance of hammers from the strings
Action screwdriver
Regulating screwdriver
Damper regulator
Capstan regulator

To make full use of these chapters on piano tuning, the student should have a piano available. He will need to put

in many hours practising tuning, and considerable time learning to regulate the piano action. The student must also learn
about the musical scale and its intervals, and should know
a good deal about the piano and its construction. All the
important points can be learned from this book.

It is necessary to put in as much time as possible in actual
practice. Enough information is provided to get the student
started; then the material is arranged so that during rest
periods he can learn such theory as is necessary.

Tuning is an art based on science; in theory it should be
exact, but in practice there is sufficient variation that it
required a group of professional tuners to decide on a satisfactory scale for an electronic tuning device. Nevertheless, any
group of professional tuners anywhere in the world can easily
agree on whether or not a piano is in tune. The piano tuner's
skill, along with that of the concert artist, is on trial at every
concert. There can be very little guesswork – the tuner must
be right.

Electronic tuning instruments are now used by individuals
and in many factories. They are expensive, and most professional tuners find that they can do better and faster work
without them. Electronic tuning is a visual method which
requires just as much practice as the aural (listening) method
normally used.

All piano notes are produced by vibrations. If you stretch
a piece of elastic and pluck it, it will vibrate, and the vibrations can easily be seen. If it is stretched tight enough, the
vibrations will be more rapid and will produce a sound.
Similarly, if you pluck a piano string, or if it is struck by the
piano hammer, the string will vibrate very rapidly, producing
a clear note.

Wave Beats

Pianos are tuned by listening for wave beats. This is a little
different from listening to the musical sound of a note on the
piano, as the wave beats are heard only when the note is
sustained. The beginner has to wait a little until the wave

beats become clear to him after the note or notes are struck. The sound of the note soon dies away, but it continues long enough for the tuner to hear the wave beats.

When two strings vibrate at exactly the same speed, they sound like one string. This is because the pattern of their vibrations is exactly the same. To simplify this, the vibrations may be drawn on paper as two wavy lines on which the 'waves' fit into each other exactly. If one string vibrates slightly slower than the other – or slightly faster, which gives the same effect – the wave patterns are different. The slower or longer waves interfere and cross the others, causing a wave beat – small pulsations of different intensity, loud and not so loud.

This wave beat tells the tuner that one string is vibrating faster (or slower) than the other. In fact, the two strings are not in tune. The wave beats sound to us as a very slow wow——wow——wow——wow – slow, but joined together: a sort of winding, whining sound. The more out of tune these strings are, the more often the waves cross. The beats become faster and faster, wow–wow–wow–wow–wow, until they become so fast that the tongue and lips cannot imitate them. If the two strings are still further out of tune, they become separate notes, and we hear it as a discord, like C and C sharp played together.

The tuner can only tune one string at a time, but he must always have something to compare it with, such as another string or a tuning fork, so that he can hear the wave beats. The beginner should now practise putting in unisons and octaves.

Unisons

Putting in unisons means tuning any two or more strings of the same pitch so that they sound as one string.

First, listen to a single string near the centre of the piano by blocking off two strings in the group of three, using a rubber wedge as a mute. There are no wave beats in a single string (unless the string is false, which will be treated later), and the sound of a single string will establish very clearly for the student how a properly tuned unison should sound.

10 Tuning an upright piano. The photograph shows the correct position of the tuner's arm, and the tuning hammer on the pin. Rubber muting wedges are seen on the top of the piano, and a felt 'temperament strip' is silencing all but the centre string of each note. Here the tuner is tuning unisons: that is, each outside string is being tuned to the already tuned centre string of each note.

Now, move the wedge and listen to two strings. If they have the same clear steady note, without wave beats, the unison is in tune. The student should now, with the greatest of care, put it slightly out of tune, so that the difference can be heard. He should then put it back in tune by slowing down the wave beats until they stop.

The tuning hammer (tuning lever) may be held in the left or the right hand, and the arm or wrist should be supported. The position of the hammer on the tuning pin is dictated by several factors as well as by the comfortable control the tuner must acquire. He must develop a sensitive control of the tuning hammer, from a firm push or pull in raising the pitch (tightening the string) to a slight pressure in easing the hammer back. Remember, move the pin very slightly – just enough to move it in the wood.

It may be that the first two strings you try, instead of being in tune, or nearly in tune, are so far out that you cannot distinguish the wave beats. If so, it may help to use the pedal to lift the dampers off the strings, and pluck each string with the fingernail. By judging the pitch you should be able to tell which is sharp or flat, and so bring it near enough in tune that you can hear the wave beats; use them to tune the note exactly.

The wave beats slow down to a stop when the note is in tune. If you move the pin past the correct point, the wave beat will start up again, and increase in speed the more it is out of tune. Wave beats are not obvious to the beginner, and he must practise recognising them. As they are easier to hear in the centre part of the piano around middle C, that is where the student should start. With practice he will hear wave beats wherever they occur right across the keyboard.

At this stage, of course, the student is learning only how to tune unisons; one step at a time is essential to become expert. Take two adjoining strings of any group of three, preferably around middle C where it is easier to hear the wave beats, and tune these two strings so that they sound exactly the same as a single string. There must be no waver or wave beat: the tone must be clear and steady. Practise this on several different notes.

After the student has learned to tune two strings so that they sound as one, he should practise tuning the third string in the group of three so that all three sound as one string – that is, a steady note without any waver or wave beat.

Making the String Stay in Tune

In all tuning there is a procedure to remember in order to make the string stay in tune. Pull the string up a few wave beats above where you want it by moving the tuning pin in the wooden pin-plank. Release the pressure on the hammer, ease the pin back with the lightest backward pressure – just enough to take any possible twisting stress out of the pin – and give the note a sharp blow. This is to settle the pin into a normal position, unstressed. The tuning pin must not be bent in any way.

The lower end of the piano string is looped around the hitch-pin and is stretched over the soundboard bridge up to the small V bar or top bridge which is cast on the plate. Between the V bar and the tuning pin a pressure bar is screwed on which presses on the strings and keeps them in place. Grand pianos may have a pressure bar *(capo d'astro)* cast as part of the plate, or brass agraffes through which the strings are threaded may be screwed into the cast plate.

When the string is being tuned, it does not stretch evenly throughout its length, but is held up by friction at the pressure bar and V bar, and also at the soundboard bridge. The sharp blow mentioned above will equalise the tension in the string. When these acute stresses are released the string will stay in tune.

In a grand piano the strings are wound on to the tuning pins from the right side, and from the left side on an upright. If the tuner uses the tuning hammer in a more or less vertical position on the upright, and with the handle away from him when tuning a grand, the same movement will raise or lower the pitch in either piano. Do not try to tune with a free arm; steady the arm or wrist on the piano for greater control of the hammer.

It is the piano tuner's business to tune the piano so that it will stay in tune for between six months and a year: hours of practice will make the student proficient at this first, and very important, step in his training.

Octaves

An octave is eight notes of the musical scale, such as C to C, C sharp to C sharp, D to D, etc.

When octaves are out of tune they set up wave beats in the same way as do unisons out of tune. This is because the upper note of any octave vibrates at exactly double the speed of its lower note, and when not in tune the sound waves cross each other at regular intervals setting up a wave beat. (This is a simplified description, but effective; the vibrations of the piano string are actually very complex.)

After practising unisons, the student should now learn to tune octaves. In tuning octaves he should tune a single string to a single string: that is, he should not attempt to tune a single string to a unison of two or three strings unless the unison is perfect.

Before the tuner starts to tune he inserts folds of a long muting felt, with the help of a screwdriver, between each set of three strings from the bass break up as far as it will conveniently go. This felt or 'temperament strip' is between 30 and 50in (76–127cm) long; it mutes (silences) the two outside strings, leaving the tuner freedom to tune intervals and octaves, one string at a time.

At this point the student should put in his muting strip and practise tuning octaves. Tune the top note to the lower note, F to F, F sharp to F sharp, etc, as far up as the mute allows, or as far up as you can hear the beats plainly.

When the muted section has been tuned in octaves, start at the lower end of the mute and carefully pull out the folds one at a time. This releases one string on each side of the fold so that it can be tuned in unison to the centre string of each group. When the next fold is pulled out the third string can then be tuned to the other two. This is the method used by professional tuners. Strings above and below the muting strip are tuned by using rubber wedge mutes, which will be explained later.

The student must practise as much as he can each day, as it is almost impossible to proceed with the next lesson until he has learned to make perfect unisons and octaves. He should not get discouraged and think that there is something wrong with his hearing. If he persists he will suddenly find that he can hear the wave beats quite well. Besides, there are good tuners who are actually hard of hearing.

The next lesson will explain how the tuner uses intervals of fourths and fifths to put in a scale.

Meanwhile, study of the following sections on pitch, strings and tuning pins will help the student to understand many of his tuning problems.

Standard Pitch

When a piano has been neglected for a time, it not only goes out of tune in the relationship of one string to another, but the whole piano goes down in pitch. It is the tuner's job to bring it up to pitch, as well as tune it.

There is an agreed standard pitch for all instruments which is now used in all the important countries of the world. This means that an accordion made in Germany, a saxophone made in the USA or an organ made in Japan can all be played with any piano, as long as the piano is tuned to standard pitch.

Standard pitch has been set at 440 vibrations or cycles per second for A above middle C. Instead of using a tuning fork marked A440, the piano tuner usually uses a 'C' fork, which is marked with the corresponding pitch of C523.3, and he tunes middle C in unison with this fork. Both of these forks are actually one octave higher than the A usually used by the orchestra musician and the middle C used by the piano tuner, but they are always used because it is easier to hear the wave beats with these forks and many people do not realise that they are listening to a note an octave higher.

If you halve the rate of vibration for each octave going down from A440, you will find that the lowest note A vibrates at 27.5cps. On the other hand, if you double the speed of the C fork (523.3) for each octave going up, the top note C will vibrate at 4,186.4cps, which is also correct.

The tuning fork sold today is standard pitch. Early this century the old 'concert pitch' was in use, and this was nearly half a tone higher than the old 'universal pitch' A435, which was also used until about 1926. These three pitches together caused a great deal of confusion among musicians and tuners.

Strings

When strings are rusty or have not been disturbed for a long time, the tuner lowers the pitch slightly before bringing them up. This breaks the rust and often prevents breaking the string. Many tuners smear a drop of oil on the string at the top bearing for this reason, but oil must not be allowed to seep down the bass strings into the winding.

The tuner then gives the key a sharp blow to set the tuning; this evens out the tension of the string, which may be hung up at the pressure bar or bridge.

It is not unusual to find a single 'false' or 'wild' string which has a beat of its own. These false beats are caused by any one of a number of different factors, such as insufficient down-bearing on the bridge or at the pressure bar, a twist or kink in the string, or the string not clearing the bridge cleanly. Alternatively, the bridge-pin may be loose or not properly placed, or the string or strings may be made of a batch of poor steel.

In tuning, the false or wild string should be tuned after the other strings in the unison have been tuned. It is often possible to cancel out the false beats of two strings by tuning one against the other, thus reducing the beat to a minimum.

Tuning Pins

In addition to the above minor problems caused by differences in pitch and defective strings, there are others which have to do with tuning pins. There are about 230 tuning pins in the standard piano, and they are set in a laminated pin-plank which is immediately behind the iron plate. Pin-planks are generally made of laminations of hard rock-maple, although some manufacturers use beech. The laminations of maple in the pin-plank present a pattern of end-grain wood to the tuning pin, which assists in keeping it from turning too easily.

When the piano is being made, the pin-plank or pin-block is drilled and the tuning pins are driven into place. They are hammered in, not screwed, and it is the tightness of the tuning pin in the pin-plank that keeps the piano in tune. Expansion and contraction of the soundboard also affect the tuning, but the above statement is essentially correct.

The tuning pins have a fine thread which comes into use only when the pin has to be taken out. However, quite a lot of turning is necessary to withdraw the pin, and this enlarges the hole, so that a pin of a larger size should be used as a replacement.

Small tuning pins were used in older pianos such as the English cottage piano, but modern pianos use a range of larger pins. (The larger diameter and length present a greater surface area to the wood, so that the pins hold better.) The tuning pins in other old pianos were rectangular where the tuning hammer fits. The well-equipped tuner can change the head on his hammer to fit any pin. Tuning pins rarely break, but when they do the stump can be taken out with a tuning-pin extractor.

9 Practical Piano Tuning: Stage 2

If the beginner is not familiar with the musical scale and its intervals, he should study the following brief explanation. This will prepare him for the next lesson in which he will learn to tune by using the intervals of the fourth and fifth.

Major Scales

Study fig 12. Middle C is the fortieth key from the bass, and the nearest C to the piano lock if there is one. It is also the fourth C from the bass, but the third octave.

Start with middle C and play all the white keys in order, up to the next C. This is the major scale in the key of C. (The key of C means that the scale starts on C.) Many people are familiar with this scale which they sing as doh, re, me, fa, sol, la, te, doh. This corresponds to the white keys C, D, E, F, G, A, B, C.

If you play all the keys, both black and white, between middle C and the next C above, this is called the chromatic scale. The important thing about this scale is that there is a half-tone (semitone) difference between each and every note. (Incidentally, all black keys on a piano are called sharps. If you have to order new black keys, ask for sharps. Musically speaking they are both sharps and flats.)

Now compare this with the C major scale, which is all the white keys from C to C. If you go to the piano, you will find that C to C sharp is a half-tone (semitone), and C sharp to D is also a semitone, which makes C to D a whole tone. There is also a whole tone between D and E, but there is only a semitone between E and F, as there is no black key between them.

If you follow the C major scale (the white keys) from C to C, you will find the formula for all major scales, regardless of which key they start from. Here is the formula: key note, tone, tone, semitone, tone, tone, tone, semitone. This is worth memorising.

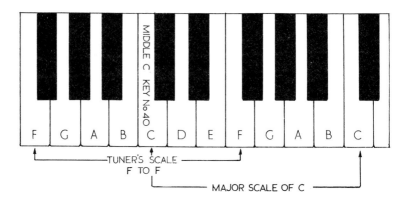

Fig 12   Tuner's scale and C major scale. The tuner starts by tuning intervals of fourths and fifths, down and up from middle C, until the full octave from F to F is in tune.

The major scale starts on middle C, and goes up to the next C, using the white keys only. This gives the formula for all major scales: starting tone or key note (which gives the scale its name), tone, tone, semitone, tone, tone, tone, semitone. There are no black keys between E and F or B and C, therefore they are a semitone, not a whole tone, apart. Start on any key and use this formula to sound the major scale of that note.

If the starting key is changed from the natural key of C to G, and you play from G to G, you will find that it is necessary to play F sharp instead of F in order to make the major scale sound right and to conform to the sequence key note, tone, tone, semitone, tone, tone, tone, semitone. Therefore, one sharp (F sharp) is necessary to make the major scale in the key of G. Try this on the piano.

If you start the major scale on F, you will have to use B flat to make the scale and the sequence correct.

Intervals

Intervals are divisions of the musical scale. Thirds, fourths, fifths and sixths are the intervals most used by the piano tuner. C to E is a third (spanning the three adjoining white notes C–D–E). C to G (five notes) is a fifth.

There are two kinds of thirds used in tuning. F to A, F sharp to A sharp, G to B, etc, are major thirds, and contain four semitones or half-tones. Minor thirds contain one half-tone less than major thirds: for example, F to G sharp, F sharp to A, G to A sharp, etc. These thirds, especially the major third, are very important to the tuner, as he uses them to test and correct his work.

The interval of the fourth is four notes of the scale, for example G up to C, A to D, B to E, F sharp to B, G sharp to C sharp, etc.

The interval of the fifth, going up, is F to C, F sharp to C sharp, G to D, etc.

The sixth is from F to D, F sharp to D sharp, G to E, etc. The sixth is also used by the tuner for testing and correcting his work.

An octave is the distance between any two keys of the same name, eg C to C, C sharp to C sharp, D to D, etc.

It is not vital that the tuner understand the construction of scales as outlined above, but it is important that he should be able to pick out the intervals easily, and this should be practised.

Tuning Fourths and Fifths

In stage 1 the student learned that wave beats are set up in unisons and octaves which are out of tune.

In addition to unisons and octaves, all the other intervals used by the tuner produce wave beats when not in tune. These intervals are the thirds, fourths, fifths, sixths, and tenths; the thirds, sixths and tenths are used for testing and correcting.

Unisons and octaves must be tuned absolutely true: that is,

the wave beats must be slowed down and stopped completely. But in tuning fourths and fifths, the intervals are left very slightly sharp or flat.

It may come as a surprise to the beginner that the piano is not tuned absolutely true. The reason is that the piano is not a perfect instrument. To simplify: B flat on the piano is the same note as A sharp. In theory, however, these notes should be slightly different, and should have separate keys; indeed there should be differences in all the semitones according to the key in which the music is played. This would involve far too many piano keys to be practical, therefore a compromise is made in tuning which makes this imperfect instrument agreeable to the ear.

This is accomplished by tuning in what is called the 'equal-tempered' scale, the only method used by professional piano tuners today. We can now consider briefly how 'equal-temperament' tuning is done.

Equal-Temperament Tuning

The tuner tunes middle C to his tuning fork (C523.3), which sets the pitch for the whole piano. From middle C he tunes by fourths and fifths up and down for a complete octave in the centre of the piano, extending from F below middle C to E above middle C. This is called 'laying the bearings' or 'putting in the scale'. When this first octave has been correctly tuned, the tuner copies it by tuning in octaves, F to F, F sharp to F sharp, G to G, etc, right up to the top note of the piano, and right down to the last note in the bass. From this it will be seen that this first octave is of great importance.

The first step in tuning this all-important octave, after setting middle C to the correct pitch, is to tune the first fifth, C down to F. This F is left slightly sharp, about one wave beat in two seconds.

The next step is to tune G, which is a fourth below middle C. This fourth is left slightly flat, about one wave beat per second. The rest of the octave is tuned in reversing fifths and fourths (up and down), all of which are left slightly flat.

The result of this treatment, when properly done, is that the piano sounds in tune no matter whether the music is played in the open key of C, or in the key of F, or B flat, or any other key.

Many years ago, the intervals of the fourth and fifth were tuned exactly true. Although the piano sounded correct in some keys, it was quite out of tune in others. This out-of-tuneness was called the 'colour of the key', but today such tuning would not be tolerated. However, this old scale is very useful to the beginner.

Tuning the Old Scale

At this point the student must concentrate on the next important step in his training. Begin by inserting folds of the felt muting strip between each group of three strings, which will leave only the centre strings free to be tuned (see p. 77). Practise tuning the first octave F to F in the old-fashioned scale mentioned above. The fourths and fifths must all be tuned true, ie all wave beats must be stopped.

The following order in which the notes should be tuned, one to the other, is the same as is used in the modern equal-tempered scale. The difference between the two scales is that the equal-tempered scale is more difficult for the beginner because the intervals are not tuned true, but are left either sharp or flat. However, practice on this old method will help the beginner in two ways: it will give him valuable experience in tuning fourths and fifths, which will make the next lesson much easier; and it will give him a clearer understanding of the equal-tempered scale, which he will learn next, and provide a practical illustration of why it is so superior as a method of tuning.

The drawing of keys in fig 12 shows the octave used in the tuner's scale, F to F. This same octave is used for both the old scale which the student is about to practise and the equal-tempered scale which will be taught in the next lesson.

Sequence of Notes

Here is the sequence of notes used in putting in either the old or the modern scale. Tune the following intervals *absolutely true*:

1   After tuning middle C to the tuning fork, tune the F below to middle C. (This interval is a fifth.)

2   Next tune the G below to middle C. (This is a fourth down.)

3   Now tune D (a fifth up) to the G just tuned.

4   Tune A (a fourth down) to the D just tuned.

5   Tune E (a fifth up) to the A.

6   Now tune B (a fourth down) to the E.

Note: All the above are white keys within the octave from F below middle C to the E above middle C. The top F of the full octave (F to F) is tuned after the rest of the scale is completed.

Now tune the black keys:

7   Tune F sharp (a fourth down) to the B which you have already tuned.

8   Tune C sharp (a fifth up) to the F sharp.

9   Tune G sharp (a fourth down) to C sharp.

10   Tune D sharp (a fifth up) to G sharp.

11   Tune A sharp (a fourth down) to D sharp.

12   To complete the octave, tune F (a fifth up) to A sharp.

The rest of the piano may now be tuned in octaves up, as F sharp to F sharp, G to G, etc, and the bass end tuned in the same way. However, one additional octave will be enough to demonstrate this old unsatisfactory scale. Pull out one fold of the felt mute at a time, and tune the unisons as you go along, starting at the lower end. This is done after the octaves have been tuned as far as the felt mute extends.

By tuning the fourths and fifths true (without any wave beats) it will be found that the harmony of most chords sounds rough. This is due to the fast beats of most of the major thirds and major sixths.

Listen to the rate of wave beats in the major thirds. Start at the low end of your first octave, playing F and A together, then F sharp and A sharp, G and B, G sharp and C, A and C sharp, A sharp and D, B and D sharp, C and E. In this old scale, all the resulting thirds, except two, beat too fast; the two exceptions, G sharp and C, and A sharp and D, beat far too slowly to be agreeable to the ear.

When the student begins using the equal-tempered scale (which will be the next lesson) he will find that most of the thirds and the sixths will come out much slower than in the old scale, and the beat rate will be much more even in all the thirds. The beat rate will increase very gradually as the thirds are played progressively up the scale.

The student should miss no opportunity to listen to the progressive thirds and sixths in any piano which is in tune, as he will have to become so familiar with the correct beat rates that he will notice an error at once.

To sum up the points in this lesson, the student has learned about two different scales. The old scale, which he should practise, has the fourths and fifths tuned exactly true, ie without wave beats. This tuning results in intervals of thirds and sixths in which the wave beats are not even; some beat too fast and some too slowly.

The second scale, the modern equal-tempered scale which the student will practise in the next lesson, is different in only one way: the fourths and fifths are not tuned quite true, but are left very slightly sharp or flat. This difference results in a series of major thirds and sixths in which the beat rate increases gradually as these intervals are played progressively up the keyboard. They are pleasant to listen to – a sort of tremolo – and make the harmony of all chords interesting and satisfactory.

The next chapter will deal with how much sharp or flat the fourths and fifths must be in the equal-tempered scale; it will give actual beat rates for both these and the resulting thirds and sixths.

10 Practical Piano Tuning: Stage 3

In stage 1, the student learned to tune unisons and octaves. In stage 2, he learned about two different scales used in tuning, and practised putting in the older and simpler scale in which the fourths and fifths are tuned true. He also learned the note-by-note order in which the first octave is tuned, and the tests of thirds and sixths were discussed.

This third section deals with the equal-tempered scale, which the student is asked to practise until he becomes expert. The difference between the two scales is very little, but the results are so marked that the one is not considered tuning at all, while the other is used throughout the world, for concert work as well as in the home.

The note-by-note order in which the first octave F to F is tuned is given here again for convenience. The student must learn to pick out the intervals of fourths and fifths. This is important.

Sequence of Notes for First Octave

First, tune middle C to tuning fork 523.3. Then tune:

1 F to middle C (a fifth down)
2 G to middle C (a fourth down)
3 D to G (a fifth up)
4 A to D (a fourth down)
5 E to A (a fifth up)
6 B to E (a fourth down)
7 F sharp to B (a fourth down)

8   C sharp to F sharp (a fifth up)
9   G sharp to C sharp (a fourth down)
10   D sharp to G sharp (a fifth down)
11   A sharp to D sharp (a fourth down)

Like the older scale, the tempered scale is tuned by alternate fifths and fourths, up and down within the octave.

Now, in setting the equal-tempered scale, how sharp or flat must the fourths and fifths be made in order to produce the pleasant tremolo effect in the thirds and sixths?

The fifths should beat out of tune at a rate of just over one beat in two seconds. This sounds as a very slow wow——wow – so slow that the third 'wow' seems to disappear altogether.

The fourths in this important first octave beat on average one beat per second. That is about twice as fast as the fifths.

In this connection it is necessary to set in one's mind the duration of a second. This can be done by using a metronome, or by making a pendulum. A pendulum can be made by using a length of thread or thin string with a weight such as an ordinary key tied to it. The size of weight is not important, but the length of thread, from support to weight, must be exactly 39in (99.06cm) long. This will give a complete swing, from starting point back to starting point, of two seconds. One swing from starting to opposite point will mark one second.

Tuning the Equal-tempered Scale

Here are the detailed steps in tuning the equal-tempered scale. After tuning middle C to the tuning fork :

Step 1   Tune the F below to middle C : this interval is a fifth. Leave the F slightly sharp, so that it sounds as a very slow wow——wow trailing off to nothing. This interval should beat just over one beat in two seconds. It is the only note in the tempered scale which is sharp.

Step 2   Tune G to middle C : this interval is a fourth. The G is left slightly flat, and should beat about one beat per second flat.

Step 3   Tune D to the G just tuned: this interval is a fifth. The D is also left flat, and should beat about one beat in two seconds flat, about half as fast as the fourths.

Step 4   Tune A to the D already tuned: this interval is a fourth. Leave the A flat by one wave beat per second.

Test   Here is the tuner's first opportunity to test his work so far. Try the speed of the major third F–A; the beat rate should be seven beats per second. The second test available at this point is the major sixth F–D, which should beat eight beats per second.

Step 5   Tune E to the A tuned in step 4: this interval is a fifth. Leave the E flat by one beat in two seconds.

Test   Here is the opportunity for another test, the major sixth G–E; the beat rate for this interval is nine per second. Try also the very useful test of the major third C–E, which should have a beat rate of 10.5 per second. Compare the speeds of the above four tests.

These tests are used to find and to correct errors in the fourths and fifths. For instance, if step 4 is wrong and the A is not flat enough, the result will be that the third F–A will be too fast. Compare this with the sixth F–D. The one beats seven to the second and the other beats eight to the second.

Step 6   Tune B to E: this is a fourth. Leave the B flat by one beat per second.

This is the last of the white keys in the tempered scale. You have now tuned F (below middle C), G, A, B, middle C, D and E. The final F will be tuned after the tuner's scale is completed, and it becomes the start of the octave-tuning series.

Test   Compare the three thirds which have now been tuned. These are F–A, G–B and C–E. Their respective speeds are seven, eight and 10.5 beats per second.

Compare these with the two sixths which have also been tuned, F–D and G–E. Their speeds are eight per second and nine per second. Note that the major third G–B and the major sixth F–D both beat eight times per second.

Step 7   Tune F sharp to B (the note below middle C): this interval is a fourth. F sharp is left flat also and beats just under one beat per second. To be more exact, it should beat four beats in five seconds.

Step 8 Tune C sharp to the F sharp just tuned: this interval is a fifth up. The C sharp is left slightly flat as usual, and beats one beat in two seconds.

Test The major third A–C sharp beats nine per second. Compare with the major sixth G–E which also beats nine per second.

Step 9 Tune G sharp to C sharp: this interval is a fourth down. The G sharp is left flat by one beat per second.

Test Now test the major third G sharp–C. This interval beats at 8.5 beats per second. If this third is too fast or too slow, the trouble must be with the G sharp, as the C will be correct to the tuning fork. Also, if the third C–E is too fast or too slow, the trouble must lie with the E, for the same reason. Make sure that middle C is correct with the tuning fork before you start, then it will be one note you can depend on.

Step 10 Tune D sharp to G sharp: this interval is a fifth up. Leave it flat by less than one beat per second, not quite one beat in two seconds.

Test Test the major sixth F sharp–D sharp, which should beat 8.5 beats per second. Also test the third B–D sharp, which beats ten beats per second. The good tuner is always testing, and is quick to alter any interval which shows up as incorrect. He does not hesitate to tune back a few notes to pick up an error.

Step 11 Tune A sharp to D sharp: this interval is a fourth down. The A sharp is left flat and beats one beat per second.

Test Test the third F sharp–A sharp. It should beat 7.5 per second. Also test the third A sharp–D sharp; this should beat 9.5 per second.

Step 12 To complete the first octave, tune the F above middle C to the F below. This octave should be tuned true, but the student should check with the fifth below which is A sharp, and also with the fourth below which is middle C, and balance out (or even out) the wave beats between these two intervals. Each octave has a fourth and a fifth which the tuner should balance out. Raising the top note of the octave very slightly will increase the speed of the fourth and decrease the speed of the fifth. The slightest lowering of the top note of the octave will have the opposite effect.

Test   You can now complete the series of major third tests, as follows:

Thirds

Interval	Beats per second
F–A	7.0
F sharp–A sharp	7.5
G–B	8.0
G sharp–C	8.5
A–C sharp	9.0
A sharp–D	9.5
B–D sharp	10.0
C–E	10.5

Testing in thirds and sixths does not, of course, stop at the tuner's scale, but should be extended up and down the piano as it is being tuned in octaves.

The speed of beats in the thirds and sixths is most important in good tuning, and although the tuner has no way of actually counting them, he soon begins to know which are too fast or too slow. If the fourths and fifths are carefully tuned according to the twelve steps detailed above, the thirds and sixths will be approximately correct, and continual comparison of both thirds and sixths will show up any errors.

It is necessary to make sure that the consecutive thirds (listed above) and the consecutive sixths (listed below) gradually and smoothly increase in speed as they go up the keyboard.

Some tuners tune by thirds and sixths instead of by fourths and fifths. The advantage of tuning by fourths and fifths is that it is easier for most people to judge the speed of a very slow beat than a fast beat. It is difficult to count eight or ten beats in a second, but experience and judgement rather than counting is eventually used in deciding the correct speed of thirds and sixths.

The beat rates of the major sixths are as follows:

Sixths

Interval	Beats per second
F–D	8.0
F sharp–D sharp	8.5
G–E	9.0
G sharp–F	9.5

In order to clear up any confusion in connection with the speeds of the fourths and fifths, use the following tables:

Fifths

Interval	Beats per second
C–F	0.6
G–D	0.7
A–E	0.8
F sharp–C sharp	0.6
G sharp–D	0.7
A sharp–F sharp	0.8

Fourths

Interval	Beats per second
C–G	0.9
D–A	1.0
E–B	1.1
B–F sharp	0.8
C sharp–G sharp	1.0
D sharp–A sharp	1.0

As will be seen from these two tables, the fourths on average beat just under one beat per second; the fifths beat slightly slower, averaging seven-tenths of a beat in one second. The beats are so slow that the sound of the note has almost died away after the first beat or two.

This completes the 'laying of the bearings'. The tuner goes on to copy this first octave by tuning in octaves, F–F, F sharp–F sharp, G–G, etc, up to the top note of the piano, and down to the extreme bass note. For a number of these octaves, both up and down from the tempered scale, the tests given above can be extended until the thirds and sixths become too fast or too slow to be useful.

The speed of the beats in the major thirds and sixths increases from bass to treble. At the lower end they are too slow to be useful to the tuner, while in the middle octave (the scale) they are so useful that the tuner cannot do without them.

In the octave below the scale, the third C–E beats at just over five per second, which the tuner can easily count; this speed steadily increases so that the same third (C–E) in the scale doubles to nearly 10.5 beats per second. When testing his tuning the tuner makes full use of this steady increase in beats, and goes back to correct any error in his work which the tests expose.

An octave or so above the scale the beats in both thirds and sixths become too fast to use. The tests can then be changed to tenths, ie an octave plus a third, or to double octaves, eg C to C two octaves apart. Double octaves are an excellent test to use when tuning all the octaves in the piano, and make for steady, wide two-handed chords all across the instrument.

In chapter 3 we found that the piano string vibrates full-length at first, giving off the fundamental or prime tone – the lowest note of which that particular string is capable. Then each half begins to vibrate separately, producing a note one octave higher than the prime. The vibration of the string immediately breaks up again into three parts, each sounding one octave and a fifth above the low note, and these in turn break up again, and again. The vibrating parts are called partials or harmonics.

If the fundamental note vibrates at 220cps then the first partial must vibrate at 440cps and each higher harmonic vibrates at a higher and higher rate. This fact is important to the tuner, as the wave beats he hears are usually set up by two harmonics whose rate is almost identical (a higher partial of the low note coinciding with a lower partial of the higher note).

When he is tuning the bass section, the coinciding partials in octaves stand out, but they are not quite in tune with the fundamental notes. If he eliminates the beats in one, the other is made worse. The best the tuner can do is to balance them out, so that neither sounds too badly out of tune. He does a similar thing with the fourths and fifths in putting in his scale, and he should balance out the fourths and fifths in every octave as he goes up the keyboard.

In tuning the bass, tune the octaves in the normal way as far down as possible, but use two octaves and a third, and two octaves and a fifth, to check and correct the lowest octave. The second last octave can be checked and corrected by using one octave and a fifth, and two octaves and a third.

There are many different ways of putting in an equal-tempered scale in the piano; but the one given in this chapter is one of the best known, is easier to learn than most others, and has been proved satisfactory for home and concert tuning by thousands of professional tuners.

11 Workshop Overhaul: Cleaning and Repairs

The Upright Piano

A preliminary examination should be made to establish the extent of repairs necessary, and to arrange a work schedule.

Take out the action and keys. Keep the keys in order, although they are always numbered (from the left). Wrap the white keys in three flat parcels marked with the serial number if they have to be buffed or sent out for re-covering.

Take samples of the back-rail cloth (bolster cloth) and the balance and front-rail punchings. This will save time in selecting the right thickness if they are to be replaced with new felts.

Use a vacuum cleaner, a 1in (25mm) paintbrush, and long tweezers, to clean the piano back and front; then wash it, using a pail of hot water with a cupful of trisodium phosphate. Do not get too much water on the soundboard. Great care must be taken to see that it is dried quickly, particularly at the back where water may be trapped between the bottom of the soundboard and the bottom beam.

Ammonia and water or other cleaners may be used in place of water and soda, but straight ammonia will lift the name and number transfers (decals) off the plate. When cleaning the plate, mask the transfer neatly unless new transfers are available.

Remove the bottom board, clean it and replace the old pedals with new ones.

Some of the following repairs are treated separately under their respective headings so that they can be referred to more

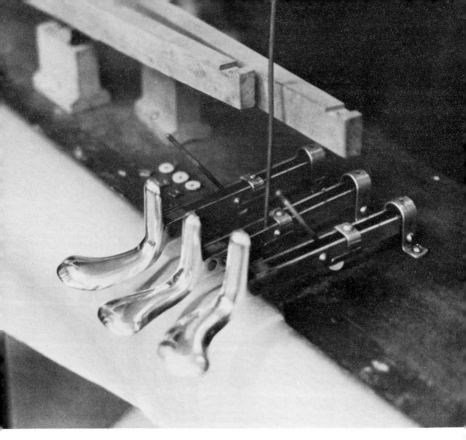

11 When pedals become worn or broken, they should be replaced. The old pedals can sometimes be re-plated, but this may be too costly. The short props on the outside (soft and loud) pedals thread through the wooden pedal bars and are fastened by the nuts and washers on the left. The height of the pedal rods (dowels) leading up to the action is adjusted by turning these nuts. Felt pads between the pedal board and the pedals limit the distance the pedals go down.

easily. If there are major repairs to be done – if, for example, the pin-plank is pulling away (separating from the back posts), the soundboard is badly cracked, or new strings and pins are required – then the key bed should be removed to facilitate the work.

A pattern of the bass strings should be made and a new set ordered, as in chapter 14. The sizes of treble strings should be gauged with a piano wire gauge and marked along the bridge where each size starts, unless the manufacturer has marked them on the pin-plank; or the number of each size of string, starting from the break, can be kept for reference if that is likely to be necessary. Each maker uses his own stringing formula; for example, a number of the top notes will be strung with no 13 wire, then a certain number with no $13\frac{1}{2}$ or no 14 wire, and so on right down to the covered strings in the bass.

Remove the strings and tuning pins (see p. 128) and take off the iron plate. If it has to be painted, use a pale gold paint.

If the joint between the pin-plank and the wooden back frame is opening up, or if it has pulled away altogether, the joint should be cleaned out with a hacksaw blade, and prepared for re-gluing. Actual re-gluing should be done after the soundboard has been repaired and re-finished, and when the iron frame and pin-plank are being assembled.

Spring-centre bolts with fillister heads should then be put right through the plate, the pin-plank and the back posts. Put one through each post, five altogether, with the washers and nuts countersunk deep into the posts. The holes are filled and stained when the job is completed. Lag screws should be put in as before except where they have been replaced by bolts.

Next, repairs to the soundboard and bridges should be carried out as suggested in chapter 15.

When the iron frame and pin-plank have been bolted to the back, new tuning-pin bushings, if required, should be driven into the holes in the plate. Discard any that are loose. Everything should now be in order to re-string the piano (see chapter 14). After re-stringing, the key bed and bottom board with new pedals can be replaced.

The action should be cleaned and repaired. Clean the action brackets, bolt knobs, etc, and blow out the action with an air-brush or vacuum-cleaner blower. This should be done outside or where a strong draught will take the dust outdoors.

Put in new hammers (see Replacing Hammers) or card (buff or re-shape) the old ones (see pp. 99–101); replace bridle straps, and bushings where needed (instructions for these repairs under separate headings). Replace back-checks and dampers if necessary.

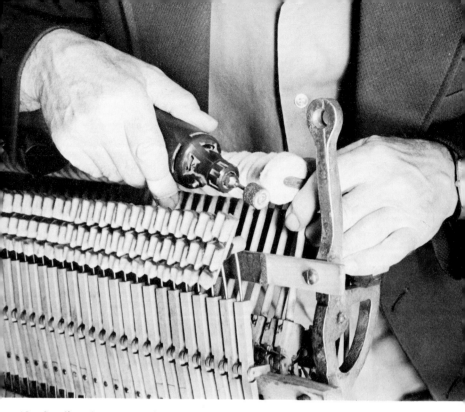

12 Sanding hammers with a motorised tool. When hammers are badly worn they should be replaced with a new set, but re-shaping can be done quickly with a Dremel Moto-tool equipped with a sandpaper drum. Work towards the point of the hammer from the top and bottom, restoring the original oval shape. This tool works fast and tends to be drastic, so care and skill must be used. Take off as little as possible, and do not go through to the wood in the extreme treble hammers. A sandpaper file (sandpaper fastened to a flat strip of wood) is safer but more tedious.

The Grand Piano

As with the corresponding chapters on the upright piano, this section is related to the chapters on the working and regulation of the grand action, and a study of one will make it easier to understand the others.

Begin by examining the piano and making a list of the necessary repairs. Note the exact height of the keys above the key bed, as this will be useful when levelling the keys on the bench.

Remove the action to a flat bench, unscrew the action proper and take it off the key frame, and prepare the keys (see p. 96) for buffing or re-covering (see p. 109). Remove the key felts if they have to be replaced, keeping samples of each, and clean the key bed.

Replace the back-rail cloth and the front and balance-rail punchings, using the samples of the old felts in selecting the right thickness. When the keys are ready they can then be replaced on the key frame and levelled. A set of grand key-levelling weights will be required for this.

Measure the height of the bass and treble strings from the key bed so that a solid straight-edge can be set up to act in place of the strings when regulating the action out of the piano.

Now remove the dampers, keeping them in correct order for re-installation later.

Make a pattern of the bass strings, as described in chapter 14, and order a new set. Gauge and mark the sizes of the treble strings on the bridge. Loosen all the strings by octaves, then remove them (see chapter 14). Remove the tuning pins, measure them and order two sizes larger to replace them.

Unbolt the iron plate and remove it for re-painting. Then clean, repair and re-finish the soundboard and bridges (see chapter 15).

Clean underneath the piano, and clean the key bed. Do not dampen it, but sand it lightly if necessary to make it smooth, and vacuum it; then sprinkle it with talcum powder, or lubricate it with a Teflon spray. The action must move smoothly when the soft (shift) pedal is used.

Replace the iron frame when it has been re-painted, bolt it down carefully, and check to see that it fits snugly and tightly on the pin-plank. The slightest movement between them will seriously affect the tuning.

Support the pin-plank with blocks or small jacks to withstand the hammering of tuning-pin bushings into the holes in the plate, and the hammering in of the tuning pins themselves during re-stringing (see chapter 14).

Clean and repair the action and tighten all damper flange and action screws.

Put in new hammers if needed (see next section) or re-shape

13 Replacing tuning-pin bushings. Use the correct thickness of plate bushings, driving them in to touch the pin-plank with a shaped dowel or bushing punch.

When re-bushing a grand plate, as in this photograph, and when driving in the tuning-pins, the pin-plank must be supported by blocks or small jacks, otherwise the cast-iron plate may be cracked or broken. (No such support is necessary on the upright piano, as the pin-plank is backed by the heavy wooden frame.)

the old ones. Check the flange bushings (see pp. 104–5) and the key bushings (see p. 106), then follow the instructions on grand action regulation given in chapter 13.

Replacing Hammers

When replacing a set of hammers, it is most important to maintain their correct striking line.

If the new hammer heads are not very different in size, each alternate head may be split off, using side-cutting pliers to split the heel of the hammer. This frees the hammer shank without having to take it out of the action. The old hammers are useless. The remaining old hammer heads maintain the correct striking line and the correct spacing while the new heads are being fitted and glued. The alternate new heads then maintain the line while the rest of the new heads are fitted and glued. Using a straight-edge, knurl the shanks and fit the heads carefully before gluing. Knurling the ends of the shanks need only be done if the fit is tight, as its purpose is to allow trapped air or glue to escape.

The exact striking line may be marked on the new heads by drawing a line along the centre of each wood moulding and across the face of the hammer, or by making a pencil dot in the centre of the hammer face. Line these up with a straight-edge, and use it to line up the height of the heels. It is some-

14 Replacing hammer heads. Alternate hammer heads are split off by using side-cutting pliers to split the heels and free the shanks without removing them. The remaining old heads maintain the striking line and spacing while the new ones are fitted and glued. The correct striking line is very important in any piano, as it contributes to the production of good tone.

times useful to fasten a straight-edge to the hammer shanks when pushing the heads down on to the shanks. This will set the height of the heels, but the striking line and the spacing must also be checked before the glue dries.

On occasion, it may be necessary to do all the hammers together: then the two end hammers in each section should be replaced first, and the striking point lined up with their neighbours. The rest of the hammers may then be removed and the new ones positioned, using straight-edges to align the striking point and level the heels.

Upright hammers can be made to order, or full sets, complete treble sets, or extreme treble sets of seven or fifteen stock hammers may be bought. They normally run 12lb (5.44kg) medium size and 14lb (6.35kg) large size. Grand hammers are usually made from heavier felt. Hammer felt is manufactured in squares 38in by 38in (96.5cm), tapered from bass to treble, and weighing from 12lb to 18lb (8–16kg) per square, which will make a number of sets of piano hammers.

The stock hammers are drilled $2\frac{7}{16}$in (61.9mm) or $2\frac{1}{2}$in (63.5mm) from the tip of the treble hammer to the centre of the hammer-shank hole. When ordering, state the weight and length required (from tip to hole), or send samples from each section showing any change required in the angle of drilling.

New hammers usually have to be voiced (see chapter 16). This is done by careful use of voicing needles to soften and even the tone, or the hammers may have to be ironed to harden the felt and make the tone more brilliant. New hammers should be sanded before voicing.

Broken Hammer Shanks

A broken hammer shank in an upright action can be extracted from the hammer head and the hammer butt with a hammer-head and butt extractor. This tool is supplied with a clamp which is clamped to the shank before placing it in the slot in the tool. Chip away any excess glue from around the shank before trying to extract it. Knurl the ends of the shank under a rough file, and fit the shank in the butt and head so that the

head will be level with the other heads and at the correct
angle. Glue the head on first, then glue the butt end. When
fitting new upright hammer shanks, the correct diameter
shank to suit the size of action (spinet, studio, etc) must be
obtained.

The grand shank usually goes right through the head, and
is finished flush. A grand hammer-shank press is used to press
the shank out. Fit a new hammer shank and flange in the
action (it must be exactly the same size) and glue on the old
head. It is possible to buy an adjustable grand hammer shank
with a long slot in the flange. This is positioned so that the
roller or knuckle is in the correct position to match the jack.

A shank that has broken with a long split can be glued and
wrapped with thread until the glue dries, when it can be
cleaned off. Repair sleeves can also be used, and even a
plastic drinking straw can be utilised as a sleeve; but it is
much more satisfactory to put in a new shank.

Re-bushing

There are several flanges in the upright and grand piano
actions, such as the hammer, damper, wippen and jack flanges.
Each flange is bushed in the same way with scarlet bushing
cloth. Repair shops usually have a stock of various types of
flanges with fitted pins which are easily installed. The points of
the pins are cut off with centre-pin nippers – but remember
that centre-pin nippers are not made to cut piano wire.

When new flanges are not available, the old flange can be
re-bushed as follows. Flange-bushing cloth can be bought in
narrow pieces which can be torn into $5/16$in (7.9mm) strips,
and the ends tapered to a point. The holes in each prong of
the flange are bushed simultaneously by threading a strip
of the cloth through both holes at once. The cloth is pulled
through to near the end. It is glued with a touch of glue, and
pulled into the holes. The strip is cut off next to the flange,
and used in the same way for the next flange. Insert a centre-
pin before the glue dries.

When dry, the bushing cloth is trimmed carefully with a

razor blade. Select the right size of pin for the hammer butt, damper lever or other moving piece, and pin the flange to it. Shrink the new felt bushing with a drop of alcohol and water (1 part alcohol and 2 parts water) and allow it to dry.

When a felt bushing is too tight, hold the flange solidly over a small hole, and drive the pin out with a centre-pin punch. Select a new pin that fits tightly in the wood of the hammer butt, damper lever, etc. Be careful not to split the wood, and use a flange-bushing reamer or file to lightly ream the felt bushing. The same size of pin may be used if it is scarred in the middle so that it holds in the wood.

An electric pin-heating device with long spring prongs can be made which works very well. It is made with a 110 volt step-down transformer with 12 volt leads directly connected to the two prongs on a simple handle. A 12 volt light bulb is mounted in the handle and connected across the prong circuit; when the transformer is plugged in the light goes on, and the technician then makes the prongs contact each end of the centre-pin. This short-circuits the light, which goes out, while the current heats the centre-pin and shrinks the cloth bushing. Bushings can be eased while the part is still in the action, but great care must be taken because the pin becomes hot at once and will burn the bushing within seconds.

Steinway now use Teflon bushings in their actions. The bushings are tiny cylinders with a flange on one end to prevent them from slipping out. When the piano flange is being re-bushed, the bushing is fitted on to a tiny projection on a slim tool, and pressed into the flange hole from the inside.

If the Teflon bushing is too tight, the pin is pushed out far enough to clear the bushing on one side. A centre-pin of the same size is roughened and used in a pin vice as a reamer. The centre-pin is then pushed back through the other way to clear the opposite bushing, and this is reamed in the same way. Finished centre-pins are used, as cutting the point off leaves a rough edge which may score the Teflon bushing. The Teflon bushings are not glued or cemented in.

Key Bushings (Balance Rail)

Key buttons are not in fact buttons at all. Each one is a bushed wooden cap, about 1½in (38.1mm) long, which is glued to the top of the key at the balance-rail hole. They are supplied in a strip and can be sawn off at an angle to suit individual keys.

Key-bushing cloth, scarlet, is sold in strips ⅜in (9.5mm) wide to be used as key bushings: bushing wedges for wedging the felt in the holes are also available. The old bushings are dampened to soften the glue, and are removed with a sharp tool. Glue the sides of the hole, and place the two ends of the felt strip in the hole; put the tapered wedge between them and press it in while holding the ends in position. Trim the felt with a razor blade level with the key top, and leave the wedge in place until the glue dries.

Another method of re-bushing the key button is to cut the strip of bushing cloth to a point and thread it through under the key button from one side to the other. Pull it through, leaving about 1in (25.4mm) which is glued on the top side. Make a fold in the cloth above the pin-hole, and place a centre-pin under it. Pull the cloth through and stretch it so that it is glued in the slot under the button and up the sides of the pin-hole. Bend both outsides up and clamp in position until dry, then trim with a razor blade.

To re-bush the key front, dampen the old bushing to soften the glue and take it out. Glue the sides of the hole, and wrap the felt strip over the end of the wedge. Press it into the hole. The shoulders of the wedge should press the felt into the recesses at the sides of the hole. Cut the felt strip, and leave the wedge in until the glue is dry. Remove the wedge and cut the loop with a special cutter or a sharp knife.

Bridle Straps

Bridle straps, or bridle tapes in the upright piano action, tie the wippen loosely to the hammer butt. The added weight of the wippen helps to pull the hammer back after striking the strings. The bridle strap also holds the wippen from dropping too far when the action is taken out of the piano.

15 Replacing bridle straps. Cork-tipped bridle straps are easily installed. Cut off the old strap, and press the tiny cork on the new strap into the hole in the back-stop. No glue is required if the right size of cork is used. Flat-nosed pliers or a hammer shank with a pin in it are the only tools necessary.

Old bridle straps weaken and break, usually at the leather tip, or they may be chewed by mice, and have to be replaced. The old tape should be cut off close to the hammer butt, otherwise the cut end may trap between the jack and the butt.

Replacement bridle straps come equipped with tiny corks which are pressed into the hole in the back-stop or catch. No glue is required, but the right size of cork must be used – small, medium or large. Once the old straps have been cut off, using bent scissors or a sharp knife, it is a simple operation to insert the small cork into the hole in the back-stop. Flat-nosed pliers are useful as they prevent the cork being pushed right through the hole.

Spring-clip bridles are used where the back-stop has no hole. These are pressed downward on to the stem of the back-stop with the fingers, and then turned around the stem into position. The tape can be shortened by folding it over inside the clip.

A third type of bridle strap has neither cork nor spring clip, but is inserted through the catch hole with a special bridle-strap inserter. This tool holds a tiny tack, and the end of the tape is pressed on to the tack. A touch of glue is added, and the tape, tack and tool are put through the hole as one unit. The tack is pressed up into the stem of the back-stop, the tool is withdrawn, and the tack is then pressed home with sharp-nosed pliers.

Instead of tacking the end of the bridle strap in this way, a longer strap is sometimes used and glued in a loop around the stem. An important point to watch is the working length of the strap. Measure an old strap to be sure.

16   A replacement bridle strap being inserted in the back-stop with the hammer removed from the action.

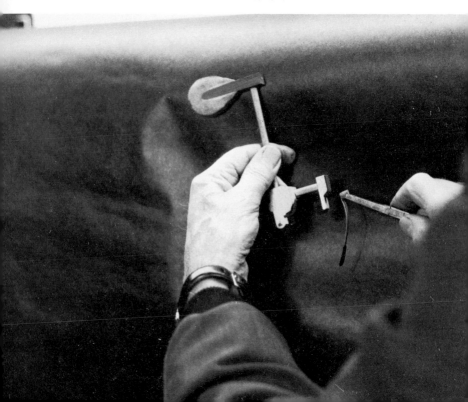

Re-covering Keys

Old ivories can be loosened with a hot iron and a damp cloth, then taken off with a sharp knife, or they can be heated with a flame or dry iron. The former method has the advantage of not destroying the ivories, which may be kept as individual matching replacements.

Sheets of ivorine used to be used for re-covering keys, and this required cutting and shaping, usually with special equipment. Now new hard acrylic tops are available, ready-cut and moulded into shape for each key, and easily glued by hand with contact cement. To allow for an even overhang at the front end of the keys, a limiting block or long strip should be made and fastened to the bench. File the notch even, where the sharps fit, by placing the two white keys together. Use a $\frac{3}{8}$ in (9.5mm) file with smooth edges. This will prevent nicking the sides.

Do not use heat to remove plastic or old celluloid key tops. Methyline chloride may be used as a loosener by painting it around the edges, gradually prying up the plastic and applying a little more until it comes off.

Ivory keys which have yellowed may be cleaned by removing a layer from the top with a flat steel scraper, or rubbing on a flat felt pad with increasingly fine grades of pumice-stone, and finally buffing with tripoli brick on a buffing wheel.

12 Upright Action Regulation

The object of the following steps is to ensure level keys at the right height, and the correct depth of touch without lost motion between the keys and the action. The complete regulation should result in a smooth, even action with fast repetition.

1 Replace the action in the piano without the keys. Set the striking distance of the hammers to the strings at $1\frac{7}{8}$in (47.6mm); ie, this should be the distance from the strings to the striking face of the hammers. The standard dip-block (gauge) is $\frac{3}{8}$in (9.5mm) thick, the width of a white key, and $1\frac{7}{8}$in long. If the hammer-rail felt is moth-eaten, replace it; if this does not bring the hammers to the correct position then pads of felt should be placed between the hammer rail and the hammer-rail supports on the action brackets. When the correct position is obtained the felt should be glued neatly into place.

The distance from the hammers to the strings varies, although $1\frac{7}{8}$in was the standard for both grands and uprights for a long time. Today nearly half the famous grand makes, both European and American, have a 'hammer throw' of $1\frac{3}{4}$in (44.5mm), while the others still maintain the full distance. Nearly all the small uprights (verticals) use $1\frac{3}{4}$in or $1\frac{5}{8}$in (41.3mm) for the distance from the hammers to the strings. Some manufacturers increase the 'depth of touch' by $\frac{1}{32}$in (0.79mm) or slightly more when they use $1\frac{3}{4}$in as the 'hammer throw'.

Apart from getting the correct factory figures from the maker, the best way to handle this problem is to set the hammer rail to give the full distance of $1\frac{7}{8}$in. After setting up the depth of touch at $\frac{3}{8}$in, check to see that the hammers trip properly and that the jack gets back into position easily. If

17 Hammer striking distance. Pad up the hammer rail with felt at the action brackets to bring the hammers to the correct striking distance from the strings. Use a dip-block 1⅞in (47.6mm) long to check the correct position.

not, set the hammer rail closer, at 1¾in, then 1⅝in, and increase the depth of touch slightly. The key should go down far enough to make the jack clear the hammer butt (or the roller on the grand) by about ³⁄₆₄in (1.2mm). This 'after-touch' makes the action feel smooth.

2 Space the hammers to the strings so that each hammer strikes its corresponding strings squarely. A string struck by the edge of the hammer produces poor tone. The hammers can be spaced by the hammer-flange screws which are easier to get at when the keys are out, as the wippens carrying the jacks drop down and allow more room to get at the screws.

If it is a metal flange action, and/or the hammer shank is warped, the hammer is then spaced by heating the side of the shank with a heated shank-bending tool, or by using an alcohol

18 Six white keys as guides. Use two white keys at each end, and two in the middle of the keyboard, as guides to establish the correct thickness of felts to use for the back rail, balance rail and front rail.

lamp while the hammer is bent and held in its proper position against the strings. Heat the side towards which you wish to bend it. A small piece of cotton wool twisted on to a piece of wire and dipped in alcohol will do in place of the lamp. Whichever method is used, be very careful not to scorch the shanks or set fire to the hammer-rail felt.

3 Tighten the key frame and action screws.

4 Replace six white keys – two extreme left, two extreme right and two centre keys. These will be used as guides to set up the correct thickness of back-rail felt and of balance-rail and front-rail punchings. If the back-rail felt is too thick the hammers will be lifted off the hammer rail. This will reduce the striking distance of the hammers and also make it difficult for the jack to return to its rest position under the hammer butt. This situation results in poor repetition. If the back-rail felt is too thin then it will be necessary later to do an excessive amount of adjustment to take up the resulting lost motion

between the keys and the action, and the front of the keys may be too high unless the balance rail itself or its punchings are also adjusted.

Back-rail cloth or bolster cloth comes in several thicknesses – thin, medium and thick. Place the end of a strip of cloth under the test keys while the action is in place and it will be obvious which is the best thickness to use.

Remove the keys and glue down the strip of back-rail cloth. Always avoid excessive glue when sticking felt, as it soaks into the cloth and makes it as hard as wood when dry.

After the back-rail cloth has been glued in position, it is well to check the six test keys to see that there is no lost motion between the movement of the keys and the movement of the hammers. When the keys are touched lightly the hammers should move. Although lost motion is largely eliminated by using the correct thickness of bolster cloth, final adjustment is made by turning up the capstan screw or dowel near the

19 Taking up lost motion. Lost motion between the movement of the keys and the movement of the hammers is eliminated by turning up the dowels (or capstans) at the ends of the keys. The hammers should move as soon as the keys are moved.

back end of the key. This lifts the wippen, and the jack is raised so that its top end fits under the hammer butt.

Lost motion actually occurs between the top of the jack and the hammer butt, but is difficult to see there; it can always be seen easily by touching the key and watching the back-check. The back-checks slightly exaggerate any lost motion because of their forward position on the wippen (see fig 8).

The next steps in replacing the felts under the keys can now be proceeded with; when they are completed, each key should be checked for lost motion and the capstans adjusted.

5   Correct thickness of balance-rail punchings is necessary to raise the front end of the keys to their proper position. This must allow for the correct depth of touch ($\frac{3}{8}$in or 9.5mm) when the front-rail punchings are in place, but the keys must not be raised too high in relation to the key blocks (at the ends of the keys) or to the key slip which runs along in front of the keys. The distance between the key bed (key slip removed) and the underside of the ivory should be about $2\frac{1}{2}$in (63.5mm). This will bring the keys to about $\frac{3}{8}$in below the height of the end key blocks, and will expose about $\frac{3}{4}$in (19mm) of the front of the keys above the key slip.

Try a medium thickness of balance-rail felt punchings under the test keys. See that there are no old paper punchings or dirt on the balance rail, as this will alter the height or level of the keys. Hold down the back end of the keys and measure the distance from the key bed to the underside of the ivory ($2\frac{1}{2}$in). Put in thicker or thinner punchings to establish the best thickness for the whole set, and, of course, use this thickness throughout the whole balance rail.

The point about holding down the back end of the keys is that the action cannot always be depended on to hold the keys firmly on the back rail. The keys may be heavier at the front than the back, and lost motion between the action and the keys becomes transferred; it is apparent as a space between the keys and the back rail. This causes trouble in levelling the keys, and is dealt with later in the chapter.

It is possible to find the occasional piano where the height of the keys above the key bed must be made less than $2\frac{1}{2}$in.

20 Depth of touch (the distance the key goes down) is tested with a dip-block (⅜in or 9.5mm gauge). Paper or cardboard punchings are used under the front-rail felt punchings to alter the depth.

In this exceptional case the keys will come up level with the top of the key blocks, and so high above the key slip that the punchings are visible. This situation requires that the balance rail be set as low as possible, and thinner balance-rail and front-rail punchings be used. Thicker back-rail cloth may be used instead, along with thinner front-rail punchings, and the capstans turned down to make the hammer shanks rest on the hammer rail.

6　The next step is to find the correct thickness of front-rail punchings. Try medium-thick punchings under the front end of the keys, pushing them well down on the oval front-rail key pins. Test the depth of touch with a dip-block on each pair of test keys. The dip-block, when pressed normally on the key, should be absolutely level with the adjoining white key. When the correct thickness of punching has been selected, put in the whole set for both white and black keys.

In addition to the use of different thicknesses of front-rail punchings, the depth of touch may be further altered by taking out the screws along the front of the key frame. This will allow the front part of the key frame, ie the front rail, to be pried up to allow a strip of cardboard to be inserted on each side of each screw, which will raise the whole front rail. If the right thickness of cardboard is used there will be very little adjustment necessary to make the depth of touch of each key correct. The balance rail can be treated in a similar way, but good practice dictates that cardboard strips under the key frame should be avoided if possible.

In setting out the above steps for replacing the felt and punchings under the keys, each stage has been explained separately, whereas in actual practice the thickness of the back-rail felt, the balance-rail punchings and the front-rail punchings should all be established first under the test keys. When that is done the test keys can be removed and all the felts put in without further delay. This is preliminary work and is not necessarily accurate.

Final levelling of the keys, and final adjustment of the depth of touch, is done by using paper or cardboard punchings placed under the felt punchings.

7   Level the keys. This is done by using a lightweight straight-edge long enough to be laid right across the keys. The white keys are done first.

Make two small blocks exactly $\frac{3}{8}$in (9.5mm) thick (the correct depth of touch), and bored to fit over a front-rail pin. Place one block under each end key, which will establish the correct level for all the white keys. Rest the straight-edge on the end keys and bring all the keys to this level.

Sighting along the white keys from each end of the piano will show up the ones which still require slight raising or lowering. This is done by putting thin paper punchings under the balance-rail felt punchings. Balance-rail paper punchings are supplied in thicknesses from 0.001in to 0.035in (0.025–0.889mm), and a different colour is used for each thickness.

Levelling of the white keys can also be done by using the Davis key-levelling device, which is placed on the key bed when the key slip is removed. This device indicates the height of each key from the key bed. In using it care must be taken to see that the key bed is level, and has no bumps on it.

The black keys are then levelled by bringing the first and last black key to the same level as their adjoining white keys. Use the uncovered part of the keys, behind the ivories, as a guide. Then place the straight-edge across the two end black keys, and bring the others up to the same level by using paper punchings under the felt balance-rail punchings. Never leave the paper punchings on top of the felt punchings. Check to see that when the black is depressed, the finger does not touch the white keys on either side; if it does this will indicate that the black key is too low.

8   Ease or tighten the keys on the front and balance-rail pins. If the keys are not free to move easily, compress the felt key bushings with key-easing pliers. If the front-rail key bushings are too loose, turn the oval front-rail key pins slightly. This will take up the wear. If the bushings are worn too much the keys should be re-bushed (see p. 106). Never enlarge the balance-rail pin-hole. There should be no forward or back play in the keys.

9   Finish taking up the lost motion all across the keyboard (see p. 113).

10   Square and space the keys. The balance-rail pins can be tapped sideways with a screwdriver and light hammer while the keys are in position. Do not sand the sides of the keys, even to clean them, as it will make the spacing uneven. Re-bush the keys if necessary to align them properly.

11   The regulation rail which holds the jack regulating buttons is adjustable and sometimes becomes loose. Set the rail so that the regulating buttons are centred over the jack knuckles, and tighten the screws.

Regulate the buttons with a regulating screwdriver so that the hammers 'let off' $\frac{1}{8}$in (3.2mm) before striking the strings. The regulating screwdriver has a socket which fits over the 'eye' head of the regulating screw. Press the key down slowly in order to see the 'let-off'.

12   Set the back-checks at the ends of each section so that they catch the returning hammers $\frac{5}{8}$in (15.9mm) from the strings. Then level all the back-checks to them using a straight-edge.

13   Space and square the back-checks. Bend the wires to space them, and turn the heads to square them.

14   Bend the damper spoons at the back of the wippens so that the dampers lift when the hammers are halfway to the strings. This can be done with a special spoon bender while the action is in the piano.

15   Space the bridle wires evenly between the back-check wires. Set the bridle wires so that when the soft pedal is depressed, the hammers can be lifted $\frac{1}{8}$in (3.2mm) clear of the hammer rail before lifting the wippens. In other words, the keys should not move when the soft pedal is used. The bridle wires should be in line.

16   Adjust the nuts on the pedal props to allow slight lost motion on the loud pedal and on the sustained bass pedal. The soft pedal rod should meet the hammer rail when at rest, and bring the hammers to $1\frac{1}{8}$in (28.6mm) from the strings when the pedal is depressed. Felt pads under the pedals should be adjusted, and there may be a limiting pad in the action which limits the movement of the hammer rail.

13 Grand Action Regulation

WARNING: When the action is removed from a grand piano, the end hammers can easily be broken by inadvertently touching the keys. The hammer rises slightly and traps on the pin-plank as the action is being drawn out.

When cleaning or working on the action, sideways pressure will break any of the working parts. If a damp cloth is used for cleaning a piano, it must be only slightly damp. Use a brush and vacuum blower whenever possible.

When regulating the action on the workbench, the bench must be flat (like the key bed) to get a uniform depth of touch. This is necessary because the key frame is comparatively light and will bend if not solidly supported.

Regulation should be carried out in the following order, though if the piano is fairly new or has not had a great deal of use, not all the work need be done. On the other hand, if a complete overhaul is required, this chapter should be read in conjuction with pp. 59–99.

1   To free the action, remove the fallboard (nameboard), the end key blocks and the key slip from along the front of the keys. Pull the action forward carefully.
2   Remove the action to the bench. Clean the piano, using a vacuum or blower and a small paintbrush. Use fine sandpaper or fine steel wool to clean the key bed, and if necessary sprinkle with talcum powder. Do not use graphite, grease or oil on the action, tuning pins, strings or key bed. Do not alter the nose-bolts (the ornate knobs in the middle of the iron plate) as these are used only to increase or decrease the 'down-bearing' for the strings on the bridges (see p. 139).
3   Tighten all damper-lever screws. Ease the damper-wire

bushings if necessary, using a piece of umbrella wire and pushing it down alongside the damper wire; removal of the damper may then not be necessary. See that the dampers sit evenly on the strings, and rise evenly when the pedal is used. The dampers should begin to rise when the hammers are about halfway to the strings.

4   Re-shape the hammers. If the hammers are badly worn (flat and cut in by the strings), re-shape them with sandpaper on a flat stick, or use a motorised tool (see plate 12). Work towards the point of the hammer, and take off as little felt as possible.

If the hammers are only slightly worn, use a strip of no 120 sandpaper about $2\frac{1}{2}$in (63.5mm) wide. Back it with tape to give it additional strength. Prop the hammers up with a thin 4in × 12in (102 × 305mm) board. Pull the sandpaper strip back and forth over two or three hammers at a time, holding it lightly but close. When carefully done this will restore the shape, making the hammers uniform and looking almost new.

5   Clean the action and keys. Use a damp cloth and a little soap to clean the plastic keys. Clean the sides with ammonia on a cloth. Do not sandpaper the sides.

6   Ease the keys. Compress the felt bushings with key pliers. There must be no front-to-back movement in the keys, so do not enlarge the small balance-rail pin-hole. The keys must be free but they must not rattle.

If the front bushings are worn, turn the oval-shaped front-rail pins slightly, to take up the wear. If there is too much wear, re-bush the keys. Strips of key-bushing cloth and key plugs are available at supply houses. Test by running the finger sideways along the blacks and whites; they should not rattle.

7   Bed the key frame solidly to the key bed. If the key bed or frame has warped, a knocking or thumping sound is heard when playing. The bed or frame may have to be sanded flat to make it fit. Some key frames are slightly concave from front to back and normally rest on the key bed that way. Four or five adjustable glides are fitted under the balance rail and are adjusted from above it. These glides (large flat studs) give

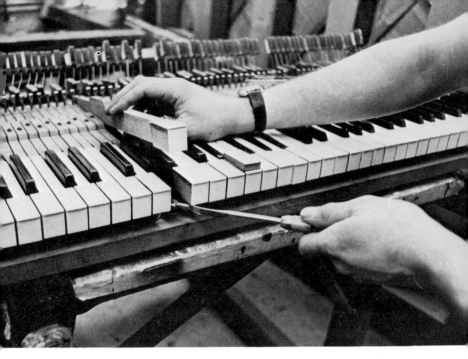

21 Turning oval-shaped front key pins. Any looseness may be taken up by turning the key pins slightly in this way, but the felt key bushings should be replaced if there is appreciable wear. The pins may be bent sideways a little in order to space the keys evenly.

solid support to the centre of the key frame and the action, but it is important that the front rail rest snugly on the key bed all the way along it.

Start by seeing that the key bed is clean, then turn up all the glides (if any) out of the way. Test the key blocks at each end to see that they hold the key frame down on the key bed without binding. The action must slide easily when the soft pedal is used.

Most key blocks have adjustments to move the action forward or back, so that the hammers strike the correct striking point along the strings to produce the best tone. This is always set at the factory. Some key blocks have adjustment screws to raise or lower the downward pressure on the key frame. If not, it may be necessary to add or take off paper shims under the block to adjust the height so that they hold the frame without binding it.

Use a 'knock stick' (a piece of dowelling padded with cloth or felt) and tap downward along the front edge of the key frame. The frame will knock against the key bed where it does not fit. Mark the places where it knocks, then use sandpaper to reduce the high spots. Leave the frame in place and pull a strip of sandpaper (sand side up) out from between the key frame and the key bed while the frame is held down. This will ensure that the sanding is not overdone; but it must be sufficient to make the frame sit flat on the key bed. Never use shims of any kind under a grand key frame.

The glides under the balance rail support it and give it solidity so that there is no knocking sound when the piano is being played. If they are turned down too far, the balance rail is raised and the action is put out of regulation. Adjust the glides as set out below.

8   Regulate the glides. With all the glides turned up so that they do not touch the key bed, start with the glide second from the treble end. Tap the key stop-rail near the glide, and turn the glide down enough to make the knocking stop. (The key stop-rail's function is to prevent the keys from coming up too high.) Do the same with all the glides towards the bass end. Go back and re-check. The end glides are adjusted by turning them down until the second end glides knock slightly, then turning them back up until the knocking stops. Use the soft pedal and repeat with the knock-stick all across the frame.

Another method is to put the key frame and the action in the piano without the keys, and adjust the glides so that a piece of paper can just be pulled out from under them. When the keys are replaced the glides should just touch the key bed; check by tapping on the key stop-rail.

9   Test the action centre-pins. If they are too tight, use a mixture of 3 parts wood alcohol and 1 part water to shrink the felt bushings. Use a toothpick to put it on, and let it dry thoroughly. It may be necessary to use 1 part alcohol and 1 part water, to increase the shrinkage, or to ream out the bushing with a special bushing reamer or a small round bushing file. Where the action centre-pins are too loose, re-pin with a larger centre-pin. Never re-pin with smaller pins unless the pin is held in a metal flange.

10   Make any other action repairs, such as replacement of rollers (knuckles), back-checks, hammers, or cracked or broken hammer shanks, etc. If the rollers are hard, making the action noisy, soften them with a tone-regulating needle. Use pliers to press spread-out and flattened rollers back into their normal rounded shape.

11   Set the height of the keys to about $2\%_{16}$in (65.1mm) above the key bed and level them. Level the keys with the action removed. Use grand key weights (as seen in plate 22) to hold down the back ends of the keys. Use balance-rail paper punchings *under* the felt punchings. There are about twenty-five thicknesses available; try nos 5, 10 and 20. Square and space the keys by tapping the balance-rail pins sideways. The front pins can be turned to take up any excess wear in the

22   Levelling grand piano keys. The action is removed from the key frame by taking out the two screws which hold each bracket in place. The sharp spikes on the grand key weights are pushed into the key near the back-checks. They take the place of the action in holding down the back ends of the keys, while balance-rail felt and paper punchings (washers) are used to bring the ivories up level.

bushings, or bent slightly to space the keys evenly. Re-bush the keys if necessary.

12 Space the hammers to the strings, first by adjusting the soft (shift) pedal so that the hammers clear one of the three strings when the pedal is used. Test this by muting the other two strings and playing the note. See that the key frame rests against the stop-block at the bass end, and adjust the limiting screw in the treble end to prevent the action from moving too far when the soft pedal is used.

Individual hammers may be moved by adjusting the hammer flange. A tiny strip of paper may be placed under one side of the flange. If the hammer shank is warped, apply heat while putting pressure on the bent shank. An alcohol lamp, or a small piece of cotton wool twisted on a wire and soaked in alcohol, may be used with care (see p. 111).

13 Space the wippens and repetition levers to the hammer rollers (knuckles). The rollers should sit squarely across the repetition levers, not to one side. The lever carries the weight of the hammer when at rest. If necessary, put a tiny piece of paper under one side of the flange to move the wippen sideways. Tighten all flange screws.

14 Set the height of the repetition levers above the jacks. Turn the adjustment screw at the centre or at the back end of the repetition lever so that the jack is not more than $\frac{1}{64}$in (0.4mm) *below* the top edge of the slot in the lever. This allows the jack to move freely under the roller for fast repetition.

15 Level the hammers, setting the striking distance at $1\frac{7}{8}$in (47.6mm) from the strings. Many grands are set at $1\frac{3}{4}$in (44.5mm) and if the manufacturer's regulation figures are known the distance should be set accordingly. If the depth of touch is set and the action does not perform well, the $1\frac{7}{8}$in striking distance can be altered to $1\frac{3}{4}$in. This is done by adjusting the capstan screws on the keys. Set up a well-supported straight-edge above the hammers, at the exact height of the strings from the key bed, and use it as a string line. The hammer shanks do not rest on the hammer rests or hammer rail, but are held about $\frac{3}{16}$in (4.8mm) above it.

16 Set the trip so that the hammers 'let off' $\frac{1}{16}$in (1.6mm)

before striking the strings. This is done by adjusting the regulation buttons above the toe of the jack. Setting the trip close to the strings gives the pianist good control when playing softly.

17   Set the hammer drop at $\frac{1}{16}$in (1.6mm). The small drop-screw in the hammer flange limits the height to which the repetition lever rises. Press the key down slowly. When the jack trips out from under the roller, the hammer will drop back on to the repetition lever. Adjust the drop-screw so that the hammer drops back only $\frac{1}{16}$in. If the hammer drops back too far the pianist can feel a 'double-touch' effect.

18   Set the depth of touch (the distance the front of the key goes down) to $\frac{3}{8}$in (9.5mm). This is done by using thin, medium or thick front-rail punchings. For final setting, cardboard or paper punchings are used under the felt punchings. To check the depth of touch use a dip-block. Make sure the action is tripping properly at this setting.

19   Set the back-checks to catch the returning hammer $\frac{5}{8}$in (15.9mm) from the strings. The hammer heel should catch squarely toward the top of the back-check. It should not be trapped. The hammer should not touch the back-check when one finger is put on the hammer and one on the key and the hammer is rocked back and forth.

20   Adjust the repetition-lever springs to lift the hammers on release of the keys. Play a note, holding the key down. The hammer should be caught by the back-check $\frac{5}{8}$in (15.9mm) from the string (see 19 above). Release the key slowly, and the hammer should rise steadily, clear of the back-check. Regulate the spring by bending it with a spring adjuster, or by the adjustment screw if there is one. There are minor differences of this kind in piano actions.

21   Set the horizontal *sostenuto* rod so that the lip on it catches $\frac{1}{16}$in (1.6mm) of the damper-lever tabs. Hold down the damper (loud) pedal, then put down the *sostenuto* pedal, and release the loud pedal while holding the *sostenuto* pedal down. The *sostenuto* should hold all the dampers up.

Another test is to hold down the *sostenuto* pedal and play all the notes. The *sostenuto* should not interfere with playing.

Play a note or notes, hold down the keys and press the *sostenuto* pedal. Release the keys but keep the pedal held down: the individual dampers will be held off the strings regardless of which notes are now played.

22   Adjust the damper stop-rail to $\frac{1}{16}$in (1.6mm) above the damper levers when keys are depressed. This is designed to prevent excessive movement of the dampers.

23   Set the key stop-rail $\frac{1}{8}$in (3.2mm) above the keys.

24   Use suitable felt pads under the pedals to limit the downward movement if this has become excessive. Adjust the pedal-rod nuts to allow a slight amount of lost motion (slack) on the loud pedal. This is to make sure that the pedal does not interfere with the damping. The dampers must be allowed to settle firmly on to the strings. There should be no lost motion in the soft pedal.

14 Re-stringing

When the tone of a piano is dulled by rusty strings, or the strings have stiffened due to 'stretch-hardening' with age, the only remedy is to replace the strings. The tuning pins are usually replaced at the same time, and it is easier if the piano is put on its back. Treble strings are supplied in $\frac{1}{2}$lb (227g), 1lb (454g) and 5lb (2.27kg) coils of each size which the technician cuts to length as he strings the piano. Bass strings are made to order according to pattern. Some piano manufacturers send details of the bass strings used in each of their models to string makers, then the technician need only give the make, model, serial and string numbers in ordering individual strings or sets.

First, check to see if the sizes of the treble strings are marked on the pin-plank, plate or bridge. They are usually marked as follows: 18 at the break, with only a few strings of this size; then $17\frac{1}{2}$, 17, $16\frac{1}{2}$, 16, etc, in groups of from six to twelve strings, ending with no 13 wire for the top group. Some piano makers do not use half sizes. (See Appendix II for sizes and diameters of wire.) If there are no numbers on the plate then the strings must be measured with a string gauge or micrometer and the sizes marked on the bridge or plate to show where each size starts.

If you do not know the details of the bass strings, make a paper pattern, using wrapping paper, so that a new set can be ordered from the string maker or supply house. Cover the whole bass string section. Smooth the paper, and mark the position of the bridge-pins by lightly sanding the paper over them until the pins show through. Push the paper on to the bridge-pins to hold the pattern in position. Do the same with the hitch-pins (where the lower end of each string is

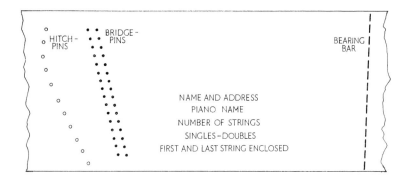

Fig 13   Sample of a pattern of bass strings made on wrapping paper.

fastened) and the top bearing pins. If agraffes are used in place of top bearing pins, mark them by making a pencil rubbing.

If sample strings cannot be sent in, make a careful rubbing of the beginning and ending of each copper winding so that the string maker can position the new winding in correct relation to the hitch-pin, allowing enough plain core wire to come up over the soundboard bridge. If the rubbing is reasonably clear he will also be able to copy the winding itself.

The pattern must show the hitch-pins, the bridge-pins, and the top bearing bar line or agraffes. If the paper is buckled, the length of string or the winding will be wrong, therefore the paper must be smooth and straight.

Write your name and address, the make of piano, the number of single strings and the number of strings in the section where there are two strings to each note. Also send the first and last strings with the pattern. If the pattern is for a set of grand piano strings and the dampers have not been removed, state that the pattern is taken over the dampers.

The entire set of old bass strings may be sent in to the string maker or supply house as a sample instead of sending in a paper pattern. Thread the bass strings by the hitch-pin loop on to a piece of soft wire. They must be kept in order, and a large punching should be threaded on in place of any missing strings.

To remove the old treble strings, slacken them a little at a time in octaves right across the piano so as not to put a twisting stress on the instrument. The total tension of the strings will be about 18 tons. Remove the pressure bar, and take each coil off the pin with a screwdriver. Cut the strings with wire-cutters below the agraffe if there is one.

Remove the strings. Then use a tuning-pin socket in a brace, or a reversing drill, to reverse out the tuning pins, and gauge them for size.

The tuning-pin hole should be reamed out to remove any rust, etc, and pins two sizes larger put in. Try one to be sure that it is tight enough but can still be turned for tuning. There are reamers for each size of pin. If there are indications of oil or grease around the holes they should be cleaned out with a solvent. French chalk is used when re-pinning to make the pins turn smoothly in the pin-plank. Some experts use powdered resin instead.

People whose hands perspire should wear gloves when handling strings, as strings can rust visibly before stringing is completed in some cases. Chalk helps to keep the hands dry.

If the piano is equipped with brass agraffes, pass the end of the string through the first hole. Wind $2\frac{1}{2}$ coils of string on to the tuning pin while it is held in the hand. Use a hand-stringing crank and the thumb of an old leather glove for protection. Then hammer the pin in, using a tuning-pin punch to protect the head of the pin.

Run the string down to the bridge and lock it across the staggered bridge-pins, then around the hitch-pin and back up to the next tuning pin. Cut the string 3in (76.2mm) above the tuning pin (for three coils), thread it through the second hole in the agraffe, wind it on to the pin, and hammer the pin in.

Use a string-lifter or screwdriver to hold the coil off the plate when tightening the string. Tighten the two tuning pins a little, lock the second string across the bridge, and see that the string is well down on the hitch-pin.

Where there are no agraffes, the pressure bar will be screwed back on when the stringing is complete, and the strings must be spaced when tension has been put on them. The end of the string-lifter has three slots used for spacing the strings.

When the tension has been pulled up in octaves across the

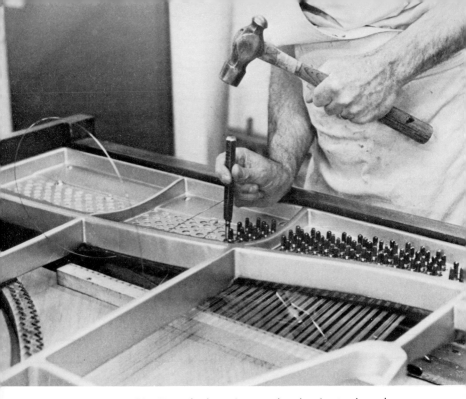

23   Re-stringing: hammering in the tuning pin.

piano, the coils are tapped with a heavy screwdriver to bring them neatly together, and the bent tip of the string is set down neatly in the pin hole with pliers. It should not protrude through the other side, but should be tight and neat so that the string will stay in tune.

When driving in tuning pins in a grand piano the pin-plank must be supported with blocks or small jacks. The grand pin-plank is not attached to a heavy wooden frame as in the upright piano, and pounding it with a hammer can crack the iron frame.

Check to see that the strings are around the correct hitch-pin, and not around two, and that the string presses on the bridge. There must be 'down-bearing' to produce good tone.

Do not drive the pins in fully at this point as they will all have to be levelled. Make sure that there is a space between the coil and the plate as they must not touch even after levelling.

The strings must be locked properly across the bridge-pins,

and press down on the bridge (down-bearing). They should sit snugly against the plate at the hitch-pins before being finally tightened. Bring the new strings up to pitch gradually, an octave at a time (all the As, etc) across the piano, in order to spread the tension evenly.

Occasionally a pin-plank shrinks due to drying and the tuning pins become loose, although the strings are still like new. The pins can be replaced with over-size pins, one at a time, using the original strings. Loosen the string one turn and take the coil off with a screwdriver. Take out the loose pin and replace it with an over-size pin, putting the string coil on it with strong, sharp-nosed pliers. Bring the string up to pitch, then proceed with the next one. Where the string loops around the hitch-pin and acts as two strings then they both

24 Using a hand crank for re-stringing.

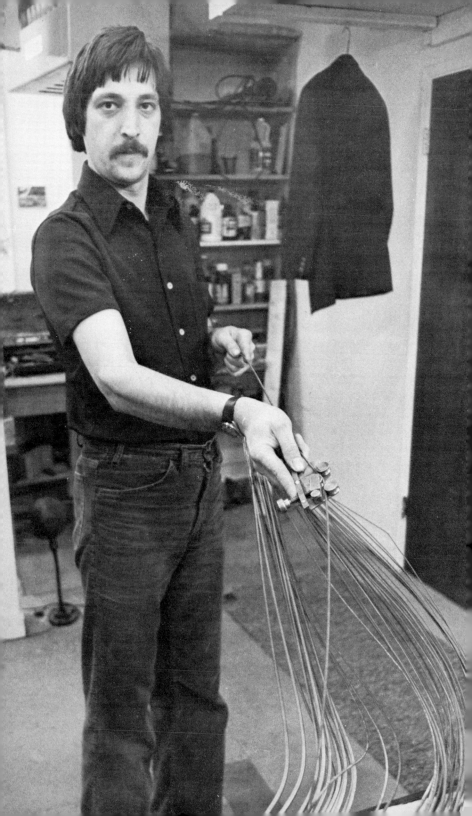

have to be done at the same time. Usually it is more satisfactory to replace the strings as well as the tuning pins, but there are circumstances where it is useful to replace the pins one at a time, and it does save ordering new bass strings, which have to be made to order.

Flexing and Twisting Strings

If the bass section has become dull while the tone in the rest of the piano is still satisfactory, it is probably due to rust or corrosion between the winding and the core wire of the string or between the coils of the winding themselves.

Older pianos had iron-wound bass strings because strings wound with iron wire gave a brighter tone, but they were subject to rusting. The strings affected can be slackened one at a time and taken off the hitch-pin. The strings are often twisted deliberately when they are put on; note the number of turns. Then flex the string between the fingers all along the winding to break up the rust. Twist the hitch-pin loop an extra turn if possible, in the direction of the winding, and put it back on the hitch-pin. This treatment often restores the tone as it breaks up the rust and restores flexibility to the string.

Nowadays copper winding is used; corrosion can occur in copper-wound strings, and usually this is not easily seen. As copper wire is softer than iron it has to be more carefully handled. One method is to tie a large loop in the string and move it along so that it flexes the winding gently from end to end.

Strings may be run through a tool which has three staggered, grooved wheels, with the same result, but machine flexing is easily overdone, and the strings kink and twist out of shape, becoming useless.

Buzzing bass strings may occur in a new piano, and this

(*opposite*) 25 Flexing stiff bass strings. Machine flexing, especially on copper strings, is easily overdone; once up and down lightly with the tool is all that should be necessary.

fault may be remedied by loosening the string and taking it off the hitch-pin. Twist the string an extra turn in the direction of the winding and replace it on the pin. Use heavy pliers to replace it, and use a string-lifter or screwdriver to keep the tuning-pin coil away from the plate when tightening the string. Twisting the string tightens the winding.

Where the end of the winding is loose, twisting will not always stop it buzzing. Remedy this by pressing the end of the winding on to the core wire with sharp-nosed pliers. Move the pliers around in the direction of the winding.

String Scales

The basis on which string scales were finally worked out was known for a long time; for example, we all know that the shorter of two strings produces a higher note. In fact, a string half as long as another will produce a note one octave higher, if the strings and the tension are the same. Also, if a string is pulled tighter the pitch goes up. It takes four times the tension to raise the pitch one octave. Finally, a thicker string produces a lower note, but problems arise here because a thicker string is stiffer, and stiffness interferes seriously with tone.

The 'speaking length' of the top string on a modern piano is 2in (50.8mm), whether the piano is a spinet 36in (91.4cm) high or a concert grand 9ft (274.3cm) long.

Here we can use a hypothetical case to illustrate a problem faced by the piano maker. If we use the usual 2in length for the top C string, we could double its length to 4in (101.6mm) to get one octave lower. The next C an octave below that would be 8in (203.2mm) long, and so on down to the lowest C which would be 21ft 4in (650.2cm) long. This is far too long, for a number of reasons.

The modern concert grand is 9ft long, and that is considered large. A string 21ft long would require a very heavy hammer, and the tone would be poor indeed, apart from its ridiculous length. If the bass strings are shortened to a reasonable length, and the thickness increased to compensate, we then run into the problem of increased stiffness, which detracts from good tone.

This dilemma was resolved by using a thin wire for flexibility, wound with soft iron wire, or, later, copper wire, to slow down its rate of vibration. The weight of copper wire is increased down to the lowest string, and the winding extends to within an inch of both the top and the bottom bridges.

This compromise of thin, flexible, weighted strings, pulled to a tension similar to that of the rest of the piano, gave the best possible tone, when all the other factors were considered. Longer strings are used on larger pianos, particularly in the tenor and bass sections, and they are pulled to a higher tension. The total tension on a concert grand may be from 20 to 24 tons, while the tension on a spinet may be only 14 tons. This added tension, combined with a larger soundboard and slightly larger hammers, contribute greatly to the satisfactory tone and power of the modern concert grand piano.

Stringing of the treble section of the piano, using a compromise between tension, length and thickness of strings (with some variation between individual manufacturers), is more or less as follows.

Starting at the extreme treble with a 2in (50.8mm) speaking length of no 13 music gauge wire, the length of string for each note is controlled by the steps or notches cut in the soundboard bridge. The bridge sweeps down across the soundboard and each notch is cut horizontally and pinned, so that the speaking length of all three strings is exactly the same. The next notch is cut about $\frac{1}{2}$in (12.7mm) below so that the strings for that note are longer.

The same diameter of wire is used for six to twelve notes and then a larger-diameter wire is used. Piano wire is made so that the diameter of each half-size (nos 13, $13\frac{1}{2}$, 14, $14\frac{1}{2}$, etc) is increased by $\frac{1}{1000}$in: no 13 gauge wire is 0.031in (0.787mm) in diameter, and no $13\frac{1}{2}$ gauge is 0.032in (0.813mm) in diameter. This gives some indication of the accuracy used in the production of modern high-tensile piano wire, even though some piano makers do not use half-sizes.

A string twice as long will produce a note one octave lower.

It can now be seen that by lengthening the string used for each lower note (and gradually increasing the thickness of wire used), a fairly even tension may be maintained all across the instrument.

We can also understand that if the tension of a string has to be increased four times to raise the pitch one octave (length and thickness remaining the same), we could not go very far before the resulting bending and twisting stresses would ruin the piano. An even-tensioned scale in a piano is therefore essential.

The string formula used for the centre of the piano is usually nicely worked out to produce a clear musical tone, but the tone deteriorates in quality towards the bass break in order to cover the change of sound which comes in with the shortened, wound bass strings. This is very marked in the small spinet models and in some console pianos sold today. Often additional wound strings are used for a number of notes above the bass break, or the break itself is moved nearer to the middle C, in an effort to graduate this tonal difference. In a well-made grand piano this change of tone is minimal, and the bass is full, resonant, and satisfactory to the ear.

One of the important developments in the stringing of pianos was the invention of the 'overstrung' bass. Earlier pianos had been 'straight-strung', that is the bass strings in an upright were strung from the hitch-pins at the bottom, in a vertical line right up to the tuning pins. The bass bridge was placed very close to the edge of the soundboard where the board's flexibility is limited.

When overstringing was developed, the bass strings were placed in a diagonal position, so that they were actually over the lower section of the treble strings. This arrangement made it possible to re-position the bass bridge over toward the right and up nearer the centre of the soundboard, so that the tone was greatly improved. The lower end of the treble strings tended to be fanned out a little to the left, and the treble bridge was extended to match, again making better use of the soundboard area.

Bass strings wound with soft iron wire produced a brighter tone than those wound with copper wire. But, as already mentioned, iron windings tended to rust, not only between the winding coils themselves but between the winding and the core wire, and this resulted in a stiffening of the string and loss of tone. Many of the older uprights still in use have the lower half of the bass section wound with copper and the upper half wound with iron. This was used to minimise any difference in tonal quality between the treble and bass strings. Copper winding is now used for the entire bass section and has proved to be considerably more satisfactory over the long term.

In spite of what has been said about the accuracy of manufacture of piano wire, the tuner–technician may come across a nearly new piano which has been strung with a batch of poor steel. These strings begin to break although they may have been tuned a few times before, and will sometimes break a few days after the piano has been tuned. The metal at the broken ends will often appear dark, instead of being clean and bright as it would be normally.

This can happen in the best of pianos, and is not really the fault of the manufacturer since he does not make the wire. But it is nevertheless his responsibility, as he no doubt guarantees the instrument against any major defects.

New steel strings have surprising elasticity, and sometimes can be pulled up an octave or so above the normal pitch of the piano if the steel is really good. Steel strings have an elastic limit up to which the steel can return to normal when released. Beyond the elastic limit it will not return to normal, but will remain stretched, and is ruined as a piano string. When it is pulled a little further the breaking point is reached.

A most important factor in the string's ability to contribute to good tone is the correct striking point. This is the point along the string at which the hammer contacts it. The grand piano action can be slid forward for removal; but if instead the treble end is moved out slightly (say $\frac{1}{8}$in or 3.2mm), this will alter the striking point of the top strings. The result will be a marked difference in the tone of the top notes.

It is not uncommon to find modern uprights in which the extreme treble hammers are actually striking on the plate bridge (V bar) rather than slightly below it. Other pianos have too much felt on the top hammers, and they cannot then strike the correct point on the string cleanly.

15 Soundboards and Bridges

In earlier keyed instruments the soundboards were very thin, perhaps $\frac{1}{8}$in (3.2mm), and often made of pine wood. The bridges were thin and light. Heavier soundboards and bridges would have damped out the vibrations of the weak, low-tensioned strings which were in use at that time.

In contrast to this, the modern upright string is under a tension of around 140lb (63.5kg), the spruce soundboard is three times as thick, with ten or twelve spruce ribs, and the bridges are of quarter-cut hard maple about $1\frac{1}{3}$in (33.8mm) wide and $1\frac{1}{3}$in high. The whole unit, soundboard and bridges, is crowned or bellied out to take the heavy, down-bearing pressure of the high-tensioned strings (about 5lb or 2.27kg per string). The strings press on the bridges in much the same way as on a violin. This arrangement of strings, bridge and soundboard is taut and resonant, making possible bright and powerful tone.

If the down-bearing is too heavy, the soundboard cannot vibrate freely and the tone is dull. If there is not enough down-bearing the tone will be feathery and light. Soundboards vary so much in size, shape and flexibility that set figures cannot be established. The making and setting of new bridges should be left to the expert.

Ribs are convex in shape when manufactured, and the soundboard is glued to them in such a way that it takes on the slight bellied-out or convex shape. These ribs are at the back of the soundboard and are easily seen at the back of any upright piano. The bridges, both bass and treble, are shaped and glued to the front of the soundboard, and they transmit the string vibrations to the board. Sound travels more quickly along the grain in wood than across the grain, and thus the ribs not only strengthen the board but facilitate the distribution of the string's kinetic energy.

Spruce soundboards are made up of a number of pieces, each about 6in (152.4mm) wide, which are edge-glued together to form the full-size soundboard. Damp and dryness make the soundboard swell and shrink, causing it to crack and warp. Usually, but not always, a cracked soundboard will affect the tone of a piano and must be repaired.

The older method of repair was to open up the crack with a saw and glue spruce shims (long, thin, V-shaped pieces) into the crack. These were trimmed off and stained if necessary, and the whole soundboard was re-finished. Sometimes cracks were shimmed with two shims, tapped in from opposite sides. A successful newer method is to open the crack with a saw, tape one side to prevent glue from running out, and fill the crack with epoxy glue; wipe off, and re-finish the board.

Each case of soundboard cracking tends to be different. It may be necessary where there are many cracks to put the upright on its back (on a tilting truck) and remove the strings and the iron plate to do the work properly.

If the soundboard has warped and come away from the ribs at the crack, they may have to be cleaned and re-glued. Screws should be put through the soundboard and well into the rib on either side of the crack to pull the two together and reinforce the glue. The crack itself should be filled with epoxy glue, the countersunk screws filled, and the board re-finished.

Ribs may have to be re-glued from the back, and the screws put in through the thick ribs into the thin soundboard. This requires careful measurement and drilling so that the shank of the screw is not too tight in the rib before gluing.

Bridges may come loose and have to be re-glued. The bass bridge may be laminated and have a cap which may separate. The bass strings will then have to be removed and the bridge re-glued.

When installing a new bridge-cap, check the down-bearing first; then loosen the strings, and pull out the bridge-pins with pliers. Tape white paper neatly over the old bridge-cap and cover that loosely with carbon paper. Tighten the strings to mark the exact string line on the paper. Remove the paper pattern and square the notch lines.

Fit and tape the pattern on to the new cap. Mark where the bridge-pin holes will be with a centre-punch. Graphite the top of the cap. Fit the cap so that the playing string side is slightly higher, and glue it on. Drill the pin-holes on the string line, not to either side. If the bridge-pins are staggered the string will be kinked and trapped as it goes through between them, whereas if the pins are in line the string will be locked on to the bridge but will still move when being tuned. Notch the cap with a sharp chisel. Drive the pins home and tighten the strings. Tap the tuning pins in to make them tight, as they will have loosened slightly with turning.

Bridges may split between the bridge-pins, and the pins become loose. It often requires careful examination to find them. Loosen the strings and pull out the pins with heavy pliers. Fill the holes with epoxy glue and tap the pins' home with a hammer. This will force the glue into the crack and make a solid job. Occasionally there are bridge-pins which are not driven to the bottom of the hole and they cause a vibration, spoiling the tone in that note. Tapping them right home will remedy this trouble.

Down-bearing

The strings on a piano, as explained earlier, press down on the bridge in the same way as the strings on a violin or guitar. This downward pressure, called down-bearing, is necessary in order to transmit the strings' vibrations through the bridge to the soundboard. If there is no down-bearing the tone will be weak, and be spoiled by rattles and buzzes. If there is too much down-bearing the soundboard tends to be held rigid and not be free to reflect the vibrations of the strings.

In order to test whether there is down-bearing of the strings in a piano, a simple E-shaped tool can be made from thick plastic. All three prongs should be equal in length. The centre prong is placed on the string where it passes over the bridge. If there is down-bearing, the tool will rock on the centre prong, leaving a space between the outer legs and the string.

There is another method. A string can be taken off, and a strong thread run from the top plate bridge or V bar to the hitch-pin. If it touches the bridge before the base of the hitch-pin, it will show that there is down-bearing.

This method should not be used when all the strings have been removed, as the soundboard and bridges rise when released from the downward pressure of the strings. Down-bearing of about $\frac{1}{8}$in (3.2mm) is all that is necessary when the strings are under tension. As mentioned previously, the average down-bearing is probably about 5lb (2.27kg) per string, which in total would be over half a ton for the whole piano.

16 Voicing

Chapter 3 on judging piano tone should be read in conjunction with this section, as it is necessary in voicing to have a goal in mind. That goal should be even tone all across the instrument, neither hard and tinny nor soft and mushy.

First of all, check the regulation of the piano action. You may find that the trouble is not all with the hammers.

If the hammers are worn, they should be re-shaped with a sandpaper file, or with a Dremel Moto-tool equipped with drum sander and sandpaper bands, to restore their original shape (see plate 12). Work can be done more carefully with a sandpaper file. File from the shoulders towards the point. Take off as little felt as possible, and leave the very top hammers as they are rather than expose the wood.

The hammers may be a little too soft because of damp or high humidity. If conditions change, for example if the piano is put into a dry room, the hammers will dry and harden. Otherwise they should be ironed with a heated hammer-ironing tool. Press with the iron, rather than rubbing, and iron toward the point. Do not scorch the felt. Iron a little at a time and try the hammers for tone in the piano.

If the surface of the hammers is fuzzy, or generally soft, they should be ironed as above, using a layer of damp cheese-cloth to lightly steam the felt. This requires judgement, as the steaming and drying effect will quickly harden the hammers.

If the felt appears puffy and the tension weak, ironing may not be enough, and lacquer diluted with lacquer thinners (1 part lacquer to 3 parts thinners) may be painted on the shoulders toward the point. Some shops use a 50/50 solution of collodion and ether, painted on with a small stiff glue brush. Do not put these solutions on the hammer points.

26 Voicing (tone-regulating) re-shaped hammers. If the tone of the piano is not hard, and only requires evening up, needle the hammers closer to the point, but not on the striking face. Pick out the most prominent notes for treatment by running the fingers up and down the keys a number of times.

New hammer heads tend to be curled up slightly at the edges owing to the tension being released when the hammers are cut. Use a fairly wide strip of sandpaper, backed by tape to add strength, and draw it back and forth around the hammer heads to take out the curl and ensure that they will strike all three strings evenly. Work toward the points and over the curled-up face. Care must be taken as there are different types and conditions of hammer felt.

If the hammers are too hard, run the fingers up and down the keys a number of times, playing loudly and evenly, and pick out any notes which are more prominent (louder) than the others. Using only one or two needles in the holder, deep-needle the shoulders of the hammers. One or two stitches on each shoulder are usually all that is needed, unless the hammers have been chemically treated. If so, the voicer may find it useful to crush the felt from the sides with heavy pliers.

Where the tone of the piano is not very hard, needle the hammers less heavily close to the point, but not on the striking face. Needling should never be overdone. The object is a clear and even tone. Whatever is done should be done cautiously, and tested continually in the piano to judge the effect.

Now, run the fingers lightly up and down the keys, playing softly and evenly, and continue to pick out the prominent notes for slight softening. Round off the tone, giving it the final sheen of a new instrument. Never tease up the felt; but the striking face may be shallow-needled with the points of the needles. Spend a lot of time trying the evenness of the tone by running up and down the keys, and only do the notes which stand out. If you make one note too soft, the tendency is to soften its neighbours, and before you realise it the tone of the piano is ruined.

If there is much needling to be done, grand hammers should be supported by a light and narrow board. The upright action should be on its back, with each hammer supported by the hand.

17 Reconditioning Player-Pianos

The player-piano is basically an upright piano, and the instructions for appraising used pianos given in chapter 2 should be followed first. The player mechanism should then be thoroughly examined.

The player operates on a slight vacuum, with bellows which pump air out of the system. Fig 14 demonstrates the working of the top action. When a music roll is put on and the bellows pumped, air is extracted from the vacuum chamber. The paper music roll shuts off the hole in the tracker bar, allowing the small bleed to extract air from the tracker tube and from under the soft, circular leather pouch, thus equalising the vacuum above and below the pouch.

The valve is drawn down by the vacuum, preventing air from entering the vacuum chamber and at the same time allowing outside air into the valve chamber and the passage connected with the pneumatic, which remains open.

When a hole appears in the paper music roll, the vacuum in the tube is released, allowing the vacuum in the chamber to draw up the circular leather pouch. It in turn raises the double-acting valve, which closes off the outside air from the valve chamber and the passageway to the pneumatic. At the same time the lower half of the valve opens, allowing the vacuum to draw air out of the passage and the pneumatic. The pneumatic collapses up and the rod pushes the piano wippen up, making the note play.

As soon as the paper again covers the hole in the tracker bar, shutting off the outside air, the continuously working small bleed draws the air out of the tracker tube and from under the pouch. The whole system returns to normal position and is immediately ready to repeat the process.

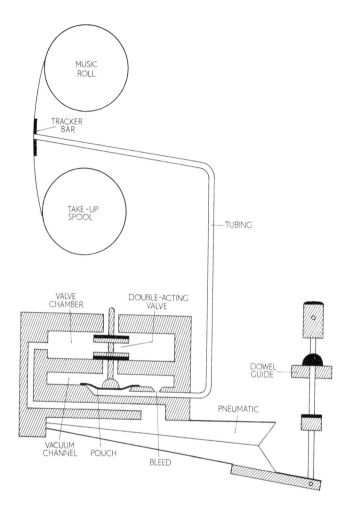

Fig 14   Cross-section of the player-piano top action and valve system.

Fig 15 shows how the player bottom action (bellows) works, and its relation to the top action and the piano action. Pressing on the foot treadles pushes open the large exhaust bellows, which draw air through a one-way flap-valve from the main channel (1), creating a partial vacuum. This first flap-valve is inside the bellows on the face of the channel.

Releasing the treadle allows large springs (not shown) to close the bellows, expelling the air through a second outside flap-valve as the bellows close. The flap-valves are broad strips of leather which loosely cover exhaust holes.

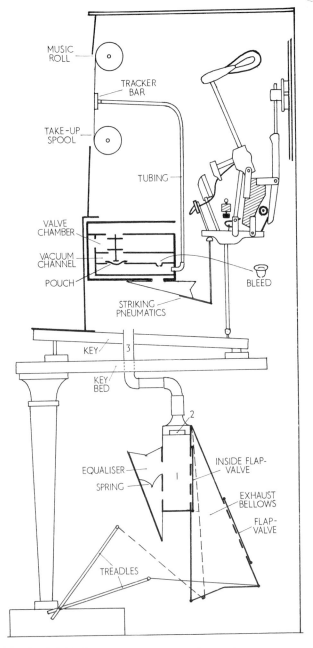

MUSIC ROLL

TRACKER BAR

TAKE-UP SPOOL

TUBING

VALVE CHAMBER

VACUUM CHANNEL

POUCH

STRIKING PNEUMATICS

BLEED

KEY

3

KEY BED

2

EQUALISER

SPRING

INSIDE FLAP-VALVE

EXHAUST BELLOWS

FLAP-VALVE

TREADLES

Fig 15 The parts of the player-piano

Attached to the main vacuum channel is a spring-loaded equalising pneumatic (bellows) which evens out the partial vacuum, making the player play evenly.

A large tube (3) is connected to the top section where it extracts air from the upper vacuum channel. It is connected to the extreme end of the top action, which is not shown.

A shut-off valve (2), operated by the 'play–re-roll' lever, shuts off the air flow from the top action when the player mechanism is reversed for 're-roll'. This prevents the player from playing backwards; it also directs the full vacuum to the pneumatic motor, and by by-passing the speed (tempo) control, it makes the 're-roll' run faster.

Normal air pressure is 14lb to the square inch (984g per square centimetre) at sea level, but a partial vacuum of only $1\frac{1}{2}$lb per square inch (105g per square centimetre) outside

27 The player top action in place. 1 pressure bar; 2 V bar (top bridge); 3 hammer rail; 4 spool box; 5 tracking device; 6 pneumatic motor; 7 top action (pneumatic stack); 8 transmission control (play–re-roll); 9 tempo control (speed control); 10 capstans; 11 key slip; 12 key block (cheek block).

pressure will operate a player-piano. For example, the moving panel on a single exhaust bellows may be 13in (33cm) wide by 18in (45.7cm) long, a total area of 234sq in (1,509sq cm). At 1½lb per square inch, that would be equal to a weight of 351lb (159kg) pressing on it. The small striking pneumatics on the top action may be 5in (12.7cm) long by 1in (2.54cm) wide, a total area of 5sq in (32.3sq cm). At 1½lb per square inch, this equals a total outside pressure of 7½lb (3.4kg) on each pneumatic.

There have been hundreds of patents issued on player-pianos, so that almost every player action is different in some respect, but they all operate on the above principle. A number of problems may arise in the action as it is used and as it becomes old. Some are relatively easy to deal with, while others require workshop attention. The following regulation and maintenance procedures can be tackled without too much difficulty.

The bleeds can plug up with fluff off the edges of the rolls, and with dust. The bleeds are in a long row under an airtight cover, but are accessible for cleaning. They are recognisable as tiny brass cups with a pin-hole in the centre, or in some players as white cardboard discs with a pin-hole in the centre. A plain pin can be used to clear the hole, but care must be taken not to enlarge it.

The transmission between the motor and the music roll may require a drop of oil. Only use oil on metal-to-metal bearings, and smear a little on the drive chains. The two narrow brake drums (one each for the top and bottom rolls) and the felt brake shoes must be cleaned and kept free from any oil or grease. They can become sticky and slow down the whole player.

The bleeds and the valves in the automatic tracking device must be clean, and the valve seats polished, if metal. The tracking device consists of two opposing pneumatics mounted on the left of the spool box, which move either the music rolls or the tracker bar to align the holes. It is controlled automatically by the edges of the music roll which, if it goes out of line, closes or opens the control holes at either end of the

28 The tracking device control box with the front panel removed to show the bleeds in front, and the pouches and double-acting valves. The large tube at the left extracts air from the vacuum chamber; the smaller tubes at the right come from each end of the tracker bar.

When the music roll goes out of alignment, air is allowed in under one pouch. The pouch is drawn up by the vacuum in the chamber and lifts its valve. This allows air into one of the opposing tracking device pneumatics, while the other is still under vacuum. The pneumatics move left to right, moving the tracker bar so that the holes line up with those in the music roll, and the control holes at the edge of the paper are again covered. The tiny bleed-holes are in continuous operation: they instantly draw the air from under the pouch, and the whole mechanism returns to normal.

tracker bar. Collapsing these pneumatics by hand will show how they work.

The loud pedal pneumatic is at the left-hand side in the bottom of the piano. It is controlled automatically by the larger square hole at the left end of the tracker bar, or manually by the left-hand button on the key slip in front of the keys. The 'auto-sust' mechanism can be switched off or on by a thumb lever, so marked, in the spool box. A line of perforations at the left of the music roll operates the sustaining pedal pneumatic.

The speed of the music roll is set by the tempo lever (usually on the key slip) to the speed printed on the roll. To test the speed use a player test roll which is marked so that it can be timed to run 7ft (213.4cm) per minute when the tempo is set at 70. If the timing is inaccurate, it can be changed by turning (tightening or loosening) a coil spring on the speed regulator box. Instructions are usually printed on the box, which is situated on the vacuum line which goes from the reservoir to the motor. A separate vacuum line goes from the reservoir to the pneumatic stack (top action). Before altering the speed regulator, see that the motor and the transmission are working freely.

Fluff will sometimes block the tracker-bar holes and the tracker tubes, and should be vacuumed out.

A pneumatic slide-valve motor supplies the driving power for the music roll through a gear transmission. A lever marked 'play–re-roll' controls the transmission, not only making it run forward and back, but also shutting off the vacuum to the pneumatic stack (top action). Therefore the piano does not play backwards, all the vacuum being directed to the motor for a faster re-roll.

A rectangular hole near each end of the tracker bar automatically controls treble and bass 'soft and loud' ('melodant' or 'melodist'), but modern player rolls are not cut to handle this arrangement. Usually there are bass and treble 'soft' buttons on the key slip. These, through the usual valve system, cut down the vacuum to the bass or treble half of the pneumatic stack, so that half will play with less power. In addition to the buttons there is a lever which operates the soft pedal mechanism. This lever on the key slip brings the hammers up closer to the strings (for a shorter throw), in exactly the same way as does the soft pedal on the piano.

The following more serious defects require workshop treatment. This work must be done with great care if attempted by the amateur.

The rubber tubing may become hard and brittle, and will crack and break. It must be replaced, but before removing any control tubing a diagram should be made which will show clearly where each control tube goes to and where it comes from. Do not hesitate to make several detailed diagrams

29 Re-tubing the tracker bar. Rubber tubing is used in preference to plastic because it is neither too stiff, restricting the movement of the movable tracker bar, nor so soft that it may collapse on short bends. Re-tubing starts at the middle of the tracker bar to make it easier to arrange the many longer tubes at the ends.

This picture also shows the upper brake drum to the right of the transmission chain. The brake drum and shoe must be clean and free of oil and grease, or they will slow down the player tempo.

of different parts as it is easy to get lost in replacing tubing if the player is at all complicated. These diagrams should include all the tubing to the bottom action and to the various control buttons under the key slip. The tubing to the eighty-eight holes in the tracker bar is fairly straightforward, and it is sometimes easier to start replacing them at the middle of the tracker bar than at one end. When counting in from each end, remember that there must be two holes numbered 44 in the centre, and two nipples numbered 44 in the stack. If the tracker bar is of the type which is moved by the tracking device, the tubing must be flexible and not so tight as to prevent or restrict the movement of the bar.

The rubberised cloth on the pneumatics may become hard and stiff and need replacing. This applies to all pneumatics, including the motor pneumatics, the tracking device, the loud pedal, and any regulator boxes which have rubberised cloth.

The striking pneumatics are glued in place, and before removing them both they and the board should be numbered to facilitate re-gluing in exactly the same position.

Using a thin paint scraper as a chisel, start at one corner where the wood of the pneumatic is glued to the board. Carefully loosen one end of the pneumatic, then the other end. The glued joint is 'started' from each end to prevent the thin pneumatic wood from splitting. The surfaces should be left rough to ensure accuracy in re-gluing them, as they must go back in the same position sideways, as well as front to back.

The width the pneumatic opens must be measured accurately before the old cloth is stripped or steamed off. Measure the length of the strip of cloth required and allow for a 1in (25.4mm) overlap at the hinge end. The pneumatic cloth tears in straight lines along the length of the cloth, but it must be cut across.

Lay a strip, rubber side down, on the bench. Put glue on the edges of one side of the stripped pneumatic. Spread the pneumatic wide to meet the edges of the cloth. The hinged end should be centred about the width of a pneumatic from the end of the cloth (enough to cover the hinged end). Press the pneumatic on to the cloth. When one side is glued, apply glue to the rest of the pneumatic and finish the re-covering. *Do not* put glue on the cloth hinge itself; it must work freely. Trim the pneumatic neatly with scissors when dry. Some motor pneumatics can be re-covered while in place, if the strip of cloth is cut exactly to fit.

The heavy cloth on the bellows and reservoir may also have to be replaced. The rubber compound between the two layers of cloth breaks down and the bellows leak, although this may not always show on the surface. Bellows cloth should be ordered for this job, and the corners are usually tacked with carpet tacks for added strength.

The pneumatic stack (top action) is screwed together;

30 This photograph, taken from below the pneumatic stack (top action), shows two rows of striking pneumatics. Attached to them are 'fingers' and rods which lift the piano action wippens and play the notes. Adjustable dowels are screwed on to the tops of the rods; limiting spacers limit the movement of the rods and pneumatics. The end of a plastic tracker-bar tube and its bent nipple can be seen at the top of the support for the numbered pneumatic board. When replacing pneumatics, take the whole unit apart and remove the old pneumatics by using a sharp, thin paint-scraper or thin chisel to loosen them from both ends. Insert the scraper or knife, front and back, where the pneumatics are glued to the numbered board.

soft leather gaskets prevent leakage. Take it apart to get at the valves and the pouches. Remove the valves and massage the fine leather pouches with the finger. Clean the valves with a toothbrush. Clean and polish the brass valve seats; use a front-rail punching glued to a short piece of dowel, and a little Brasso.

The more sophisticated type of player has two sets of valves, a primary and a secondary set. This was designed to make the player action faster. When cleaning and adjusting the valves both sets should be done. The primary valves should open about $\frac{1}{32}$in (0.8mm) and the secondary valves $\frac{1}{16}$in (1.6mm).

Player test rolls are available which test the playing and repetition of every note. These test the player-piano's efficiency in handling massive chords, the performance of the motor and transmission, the tracking device, the loud pedal, and the soft and loud controls.

A preliminary test is often made by the player repairman. No music roll is used. The tempo is set at zero, and the 'play–re-roll' lever is set at 'play'. He pumps hard and fast, and watches the piano hammers.

The hammers should all rise promptly if the player is in good condition, although all the eighty-eight valves will be open and the pneumatics connected to the vacuum. They may rise slowly, only some may rise, or they may not rise at all. Their performance helps the repairman to decide where the real trouble lies.

In using the test roll, if a hammer stays up it will indicate that there is a leak in the tracker tube. If the note does not repeat, the bleed must be blocked. If the note does not play, the cloth on the striking pneumatic may be perished and stiff. If so, probably all the pneumatics will be in the same state. Reach down at the ends of the stack to feel the pneumatics, or remove the top section and examine them all. If the player is hard to pump (breathless), the valve seats may be dirty and leaking, or the bellows, or their flap-valves, may be leaking.

Listen for leaks. Listening through a piece of tubing sometimes helps to pinpoint leaks. Tubes which have broken or

31 A small type of player-piano bottom action showing the usual two feeder bellows attached to the pedals. Long V-shaped bellows springs hold them closed. White leather flap-valves are attached at the lower end and stretched flat by the wire tension spring at the opposite end. The tension springs can be slipped out of the wooden end-blocks, and the flap-valves manipulated to soften them so that they will lie flat.

The spring-loaded reservoir pneumatic which extends across the full width of the action is seen at the back near the top. Large rubber hose attaches to the two nipples. drawing air from the motor and from the pneumatic stack (top action). The angular block at the top holds the action in position when in the piano.

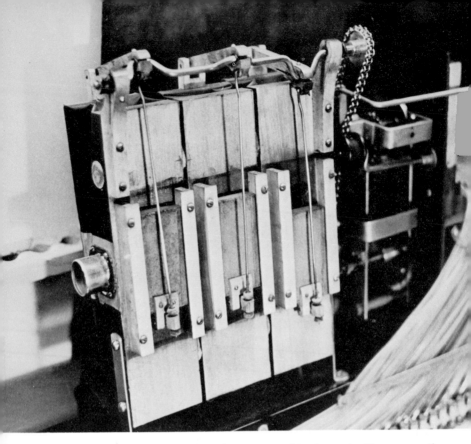

32 One type of pneumatic motor, with three double pneumatics. When the top pneumatic is open, the lower one is closed. The slide-valve allows air into each pneumatic as it opens. The two outside pneumatics are screwed to the centre one with long screws which are deeply countersunk and sealed by a circular piece of pneumatic cloth. Rubber spacing washers separate the three sections. The large nipple at the end connects with the vacuum; short pieces of similar-diameter tubing connect all three double pneumatics. The crankshaft and its supports, the connecting rods (bars), and the flanges on each top pneumatic are all shown. The chain drive operates the transmission and the music rolls.

Before dismantling the motor, number all parts, making small marks to locate screw-holes after re-covering the pneumatics.

come off the nipple will make a leaking sound, as well as interfering with efficient operation. For instance, a leak in the control tube of the loud pedal pneumatic will cause the loud pedal to be on all the time. Trace the leak by squeezing the tube at various points while watching the loud pedal pneumatic. The leak may be at the manual control button; its spring may be out of position or its leather seal defective, allowing air into the tube leading to the pneumatic. There may be two tubes to the pneumatic, one from the manual button and one from the tracker bar, or a Y nipple may connect these two with a single tube to the pneumatic. Careful and thorough examination pays off well in player repair work.

To test the bottom action, take it out and seal all the nipples, both large and small. Pump the pedals until the reservoir is collapsed. The spring-loaded reservoir should return to position slowly, which will indicate that the bellows fabric is in good condition and the large leather flap-valves are not leaking.

When overhauling the motor, remove it from the stack and unscrew the supports to the crankshaft. Unscrew and tap off the flanges on the pneumatics which hold the connecting rods or bars. Slide out the slide-valves and remove the crankshaft. Number and take off supports, valves and connecting bars. Clean all felt bushings. Leave them clean; use no oil or grease. Polish the crankshaft. Sand the slide-valves and their seats with fine sandpaper, and burnish them with dry powdered graphite.

When re-covering the motor pneumatics, make sure that they will open to the full extent, and not act as a brake on the motor. If the fabric is cut too wide, the folds will be too thick and again will act as a brake. The motor pneumatics need not be re-covered with the heavier motor cloth, as the thinner pneumatic cloth is strong enough and much more flexible. Be sure to measure the full width the pneumatic opens, allowing for creasing, before stripping off its original covering.

Glossary

Action The mechanism between the keys and the strings

Action centres Bushed centre-pins, usually in flanges

Acrylic A type of plastic used for key tops

After-touch The distance the key goes down after the jack escapes, measured by the small amount by which the jack clears the hammer butt

Aliquot bars or plates Movable bars placed on the iron plate between hitch-pins and bridge, designed to augment harmonics. The length of string between the bridge and the aliquot bar should sound a harmonic of the tuned section of the string

Aliquot system System whereby a fourth string is positioned above the three strings of each note to build harmonics; used by Bluthner

Baby grand A small grand 5ft (152cm) or less in length

Back-check Padded block which catches the back-stop on the hammer butt, preventing the hammer from blubbering

Back-stop Part integral with hammer butt (see above); also holds replacement cork-tipped bridle straps

Barrel The knuckle or roller on grand hammer shanks

Billings flange A type of metal flange

Birdcage action An old type of overdamper action in which the dampers operate above the hammers

Bleeds Small vents which permit repetition in player-piano actions

Blubbering Bouncing of the hammer against the strings; indicates that the back-check is not working

Bolster cloth A strip of thick, dark green, felt-like cloth (baize) used on the back rail under the keys

Bracket bolt One of three or four large bolts, with plated knurled nuts, which hold the top of the upright action in place

Break The division between the treble and bass strings and treble and bass hammers

Bridle strap A narrow, leather-tipped tape which ties the upright wippen to the hammer, hastening its return

Bushing The felt lining of a bearing

Butt The base in which the upright hammer shank and back-stop are set

Cabinet grand An obsolete name for any upright having three strings to each note throughout the treble

Capstan A brass, capstan-shaped adjustable screw on the piano key

Carding Smoothing or re-shaping piano hammers with sandpaper

Cheek blocks Key blocks at the ends of the keyboard

Chipping up Roughly tuning a newly strung piano, using a wooden plectrum or chip

Centre pedal Pedal placed between the soft and sustaining pedals, controlling a sustained bass or *sostenuto* mechanism

Centre-pin Small hinge-pin joining the stationary flange and working parts in an action

Damper The felt-padded block which stops the vibration of the strings

Damper lever Part of the damper unit

Damper spoon Spoon-shaped part set in the end of the wippen which pushes out the lower end of the upright damper lever

Damper stop-rail A light rail with felt strip which prevents the weighted damper lever in the grand action from rising too high or limits the movement of the upright dampers

Decal A transfer name usually put on the fallboard (keyboard lid)

Dip-block A block gauge used for measuring the depth the white keys go down ($\frac{3}{8}$in or 9.5mm) and the distance of the upright hammers from the strings

Direct action The normal type of upright action in which the keys fit directly under the action

Down-bearing The downward pressure exerted by taut strings on the soundboard bridges

Down-bearing tool An E-shaped piece of thick plastic with all three prongs of equal length. The centre prong is placed on the string at the high point where it goes over the bridge; if the tool rocks on the string, it indicates that there is down-bearing

Drop action An indirect action in a small piano which is dropped down behind and below the shortened keys

Fallboard The hinged lid which covers the keys

Flange The stationary part of the hinge which holds the centre-pin on which the working parts swing

Fly Another name for the jack

Forte Loud

Glides Large metal buttons on which the grand action slides when the soft pedal is used

Graphite A dry black lubricant which comes in powder or stick form. A lead pencil may be used as a substitute to stop squeaks in damper or hammer-spring punchings

Hammer iron A special tool for ironing piano hammers to harden them

Hammer rail The long bar in the upright action against which the hammer shanks rest; sets the distance from the hammers to the strings (hammer blow)

Hammer travel The movement of the hammer towards the strings which should be a straight line

Harmonics The higher sounds produced by an aliquot part or segment of a vibrating string

Harpsichord A stringed instrument in which the strings are mechanically plucked, and from which the grand piano took its shape

Indirect action An action placed behind and below the keys in a small piano, in which a wire or wooden sticker pulls up the wippen instead of pushing it up as in a direct action

Ironbars Bars used to strengthen the wooden frame of the piano before the cast-iron plate was invented

Iron frame The cast-iron plate which supports and is supported by the wooden frame; together they withstand the total stress of the piano strings

Jack The action part that pushes the hammer up to the strings, and is tripped out of place before the hammer can jam against the strings

Jack cushion Small square block of red felt which cushions the jack on its return to its normal position under the hammer butt

Key bed The base in the piano on which the key and action units rest

Key blocks The cheek blocks at the ends of the keyboard

Key-bushing cloth Hard-wearing scarlet cloth usually ready-cut into strips for re-bushing keys

Key-bushing wedge A wooden wedge used as a clamp when gluing in key bushings

Key button A short wooden piece glued on top of the key and bushed to take the balance-rail pin

Key dip The depth of touch: the distance the front of the key goes down

Key slip The long, slim wooden strip in front of the keys, usually fastened to the key bed in the grand or the key frame in the upright

Key stop-rail A light rail fastened over the keys in a grand piano which prevents them from rising too high. The fall strip in the upright performs the same function

Knock-stick A padded stick used to knock on the grand key frame to tell whether it is warped

Knuckle The roller or barrel-shaped cushion on the underside of the grand hammer shank which takes the upward thrust of the jack

Laminated board Thin sheets of wood glued together transversely to form a board or plank, as a pin-plank

Leads Small round or flat weights used in weighting keys

Let-off Another name for the trip: escapement of the jack after raising the hammer

Lost motion Slack between the keys and the upright piano action

Loud pedal The sustaining pedal which holds all the dampers off the strings

Metronome An instrument for beating time in music; can be used for counting wave beats in tuning

Muffler A strip of felt placed between the hammers and the strings to muffle the tone

Muting felt A felt strip used for muting or blocking off strings to allow the tuner to tune one string at a time

Overtones Less prominent harmonics

Partials Segments of a vibrating string which produce harmonics or overtones

Particle-board A board made of compressed wood particles or chips

Pedal lyre The support structure for the grand pedals

Pedal box The box at the bottom of the pedal lyre which holds the pedals

Piano Soft

Pin-plank The laminated board behind the plate into which the tuning pins are driven

Pitch The position of a note on the musical scale, established by the number of vibrations per second. Standard pitch A440 means that the note A above middle C vibrates at 440 cycles per second

Pneumatic motor The pneumatic slide-valve motor in a player-piano which drives the music-roll spools

Pneumatic stack The two or three ranks of striking pneumatics in the top player action

Pneumatic striking *See* Striking pneumatic

Pouches Soft, thin leather disc-shaped pouches which are drawn up by vacuum in the player-piano action, raising double-acting valves which control the opening or collapsing of the pneumatics

Pressure bar A metal bar screwed on over the upright strings above the V bar or top bridge

Punching A disc or washer of felt or paper used under the piano keys

Regulation Adjustment

Regulation button The adjustable button or dowel on which the toe of the jack trips

Regulation rail The rail which holds eighty-eight regulation buttons (see above)

Ribs The shaped supporting pieces glued to the back of the soundboard

Roller The barrel-shaped cushion on the underside of the grand hammer shank

Serial number The number stamped on each piano when it is made, thereby indicating the year of manufacture

Shims Thin cardboard or wood pieces used to raise or lower the balance rail or to fill a crack in a soundboard

Sostenuto A mechanism, controlled by the centre or *sostenuto* pedal, which enables the pianist to sustain individual notes or chords

Soundboard steel A thin, flat, flexible steel piece used with a cloth for cleaning the soundboard in a grand piano

Standard pitch A440: when A above middle C vibrates at 440 cycles per second

Stencil A trademark name other than the manufacturer's name

Stitching Pressing the voicing needles deep into the hammer shoulders

Stretch-hardening Hardening and stiffening of steel string with age and stretching; similar to work-hardening or fatigue in steel

Striking pneumatic One of the eighty-eight small pneumatics (bellows) in the player-piano which, on collapsing, raise the wippen in the piano action, thereby making the note play

Sympathetic vibration An induced vibration which makes objects rattle or strings vibrate in sympathy

Teflon bushing A type of plastic bushing used in Steinway piano actions

Temperament strip *See* Muting felt

Tone-regulating needles Needles set in a handle, used to soften piano hammers

Tone regulation Voicing, carried out by deep-needling the shoulders of piano hammers to soften them

Tracking device A device composed of two opposing pneumatics which moves either the tracker bar or the music roll on a player-piano to keep the holes in line

Transmission The 'roll–re-roll' gear assembly on a player-piano, complete with chain drives and brakes

Trap-work The pedal levers, etc, connected to the piano pedals

Trip Escapement of the jack after raising the hammer to the strings

Tuning hammer A special tuning lever for turning the tuning pins; originally a T-shaped tuning tool

Tuning-pin bushings Wooden bushings which are hammered into the holes in the plate, and through which the tuning pins protrude; designed to support the tuning pins

Tuning-pin extractor A special tool for extracting broken tuning pins

Tuning-pin socket Tool used in a brace or reversible drill to take out tuning pins

Valve (double-acting) Double valve which controls the flow of air into or out of the striking pneumatics of a player-piano causing them to open or collapse

V bar The small V-shaped casting on the iron plate which acts as a top bridge

Voicer The technician who evens out the tone of a piano by needling the hammers

Weight of touch The finger pressure or weight required to sound a note on the piano

Wippen The lever in the grand and upright piano actions which carries the jack

Appendix I:
Piano Manufacturers

Piano Companies Taken Over By Others

G. Bechstein Piano Co, Germany, by Baldwin Piano & Organ Co, USA

Bosendorfer Piano Co, Vienna, by Jasper Corp (parent company of Kimball Piano & Organ Co), Jasper, Indiana, USA

Everett Piano Co, South Haven, Michigan, USA, by Yamaha Piano Co, Japan

Mason & Risch Piano Co, Toronto, by Winter & Co, who formed the Canadian Piano Co

Sherlock-Manning Piano Co, Clinton, Ontario, by W. D. Heintzman (formerly of Heintzman & Co, Toronto)

Steinway and Sons, New York and Hamburg, Germany, by Columbia Broadcasting System (CBS)

Willis & Co, Montreal, ceased production and were re-started under the same name by a new group of businessmen

Winter & Co, USA, are now Aeolian Corp, New York

The following are all controlled by Aeolian American Corp (a division of Aeolian Corp): Chickering & Sons; J. & C. Fischer; Mason & Hamlin; Wm Knabe; Geo. Steck; Weber Piano Co

Selected Pianos (in alphabetical order)

Highest-Grade Grand Pianos	*Grand Pianos Graded Excellent*
Baldwin, USA	Chickering, USA
Bechstein, Germany	Kawai, Japan
Bluthner, East Germany	Wm Knabe, USA
Bosendorfer, Austria	Sohmer, USA
Grotrian-Steinweg, Germany	Yamaha, Japan
Mason & Hamlin, USA	
Steinway, Germany	
Steinway, New York	

High-Grade European   *Selected Uprights*
Uprights

Bechstein, Germany   Everett, USA
Bluthner, East Germany   Heintzman, Canada
Alfred Knight, England   Kawai, Japan
Sauter, Germany   Sauter, Germany
Schimmel, Germany   Sohmer, USA
                                Yamaha, Japan

Prices of these pianos give some indication of their standing

Appendix II:
Piano Data

Music Wire

Music wire gauge no	Diameter in inches	Footage per pound	Breaking point
13	0.031	391	270
13½	0.032	366	285
14	0.033	330	300
14½	0.034	300	315
15	0.035	290	330
15½	0.036	285	345
16	0.037	275	360
16½	0.038	260	375
17	0.039	248	390
17½	0.040	234	405
18	0.041	223	425
18½	0.042	212	455
19	0.043	200	475
19½	0.044	195	495
20	0.045	182	515
21	0.047	165	550

Elastic limit approximately 70 per cent of breaking point

Tuning-pin sizes

Size	Diameter in inches	Length in inches
2/0	0.281	$2\frac{1}{2}, 2\frac{3}{8}, 2\frac{1}{4}$
3/0	0.286	$2\frac{1}{2}, 2\frac{3}{8}, 2\frac{1}{4}$
4/0	0.291	$2\frac{1}{2}, 2\frac{3}{8}, 2\frac{1}{4}$
5/0	0.296	$2\frac{1}{2}, 2\frac{3}{8}, 2\frac{1}{4}$
6/0	0.301	$2\frac{1}{2}, 2\frac{3}{8}, 2\frac{1}{4}$

Bridge-pin sizes

Size	Diameter in inches	Length in inches
6	0.078	$\frac{3}{4}$
7	0.086	$\frac{3}{4}$
8	0.096	$\frac{3}{4}$
9	0.109	$\frac{3}{4}$

Centre-pin sizes

Size	Diameter in inches
18	0.046
$18\frac{1}{2}$	0.047
19	0.048
$19\frac{1}{2}$	0.049
20	0.050
$20\frac{1}{2}$	0.051
21	0.052
$21\frac{1}{2}$	0.053
22	0.054
$22\frac{1}{2}$	0.055
23	0.056
$23\frac{1}{2}$	0.0575
24	0.059
$24\frac{1}{2}$	0.061
25	0.063

Key-pin sizes

Type	Diameter in inches	Length in inches
Balance-rail (regular round)	0.145	2
Balance-rail (over-size round)	0.160	2
Front-rail (oval)		$1\frac{1}{2}$

Appendix III:
Metric Conversion Tables

			Ounces	Grammes
1 ounce	=	28.349 grammes	1	28.349
1 gramme	=	0.035 ounces	$1\frac{1}{4}$	35.436
1 inch	=	25.4 millimetres	$1\frac{1}{3}$	37.799
1 foot	=	304.8 millimetres	$1\frac{1}{2}$	42.524
1 millimetre	=	0.0394 inches	$1\frac{2}{3}$	47.248
1 metre	=	3.281 feet	$1\frac{3}{4}$	49.610
			2	56.698
			$2\frac{1}{4}$	63.785
			$2\frac{1}{2}$	70.873
			$2\frac{3}{4}$	77.960
			3	84.047

Inches	Millimetres	Inches	Millimetres
$\frac{1}{64}$	0.397	1	25.400
$\frac{1}{32}$	0.794	$1\frac{1}{8}$	28.575
$\frac{1}{16}$	1.588	$1\frac{1}{4}$	31.750
$\frac{1}{8}$	3.175	$1\frac{3}{8}$	34.925
$\frac{3}{16}$	4.763	$1\frac{1}{2}$	38.100
$\frac{7}{32}$	5.556	$1\frac{5}{8}$	41.275
$\frac{1}{4}$	6.350	$1\frac{3}{4}$	44.450
$\frac{5}{16}$	7.938	$1\frac{7}{8}$	47.625
$\frac{3}{8}$	9.525	2	50.800
$\frac{7}{16}$	11.113	$2\frac{5}{16}$	58.738
$\frac{1}{2}$	12.700	$2\frac{3}{8}$	60.325
$\frac{9}{16}$	14.288	$2\frac{7}{16}$	61.913
$\frac{5}{8}$	15.875	$2\frac{1}{2}$	63.500
$\frac{11}{16}$	17.463	$2\frac{9}{16}$	65.088
$\frac{3}{4}$	19.050	$2\frac{5}{8}$	66.675
$\frac{13}{16}$	20.638	$2\frac{3}{4}$	69.850
$\frac{7}{8}$	22.225	$2\frac{7}{8}$	73.025
$\frac{15}{16}$	23.813	3	76.200

Further Reading

Baines, Anthony (ed, for the Galpin Society), *Musical Instruments through the Ages* (Walker, New York, Faber, London, and Penguin, London, 1966)

Benade, Arthur H., *Horns, Strings and Harmony* (Anchor Books, Garden City, New York, 1960)

Braid White, William, *Piano Tuning and Allied Arts* (Tuners' Supply Co, Somerville, Mass, 1978; available in the UK from Fletcher & Newman, Bridge Works, 134 New North Road, London N1 6ST, or Heckscher & Co, 75 Bayham Street, London NW1 0AA)

Clemenicic, Rene, *Old Musical Instruments* (Putnam, New York, and Weidenfeld & Nicolson, London, 1968)

Dolge, Alfred, *Pianos and their Makers* (1911; reprinted Dover, New York, 1972)

Keyboard Instruments (Metropolitan Museum of Art, New York)

McFerrin, W. V., *The Piano – Its Acoustics* (Tuners' Supply Co, Somerville, Mass, 1972)

Piano Action Handbook (Piano Technicians' Guild, Seattle, Wash, 1971)

Pierce, Bob, *Pierce's Piano Atlas* (successor to *The Original Mechel's Atlas*) (Pierce, Long Beach, California, 1977; available in the UK from Fletcher & Newman or Heckscher & Co)

Reblitz, Arthur A., *Piano Servicing, Tuning and Rebuilding* (Vestal Press, New York, 1976; available in the UK from Fletcher & Newman or Heckscher & Co)

Rice Hollis, Helen, *The Piano* (David & Charles, Newton Abbot, 1975)

Sumner, William Leslie, *The Pianoforte* (Macdonald, London, 1966)

Index